EMOTION CONCEPTS
OF THE IBANS
IN SARAWAK

LILLY METOM

PARTRIDGE

A Penguin Random House Company

ISBN: Hardcover   978-1-4828-9732-6
             Softcover   978-1-4828-9731-9
             Ebook   978-1-4828-9733-3

To order additional copies of this book, contact
Toll Free 800 101 2657 (Singapore)
Toll Free 1 800 81 7340 (Malaysia)
orders.singapore@partridgepublishing.com

www.partridgepublishing.com/singapore

In Memory of
Professor Vin D'Cruz (1933-2008)

TABLE OF CONTENTS

CHAPTER V: CONCLUSION

PREFACE

The emotion concepts of the Iban community in Sarawak are different from other cultures in Malaysia, although there is a close resemblance with those of the Malays. The different way of expressing emotions is closely related to the Ibans' unique cultural values, which are still persevered in this speech community despite modernization.

This book is an outcome of the research that I conducted in 2000. The study argues that, because terminologies of emotion concepts are culture-specific in Iban, drawing their meaning from the context of the Ibans' historical and cultural background, they cannot be simply explained through English words, or else the explanation will be imposed by ethnocentric bias. The interpretations and explications of the emotion concepts in this book illustrate why and how this is so. Hence, the research falls within the area of linguistics called pragmatics, which deals with meaning in context.

In analysing the Iban emotion concepts, the study utilized Natural Semantic Metalanguage (NSM), which is an analytical tool developed and elaborated by Anna Wierzbicka (1991), and the Concrete/Abstract Cultural Continuum framework, that is a framework developed by J. Vin D'Cruz and G. Tham (1993), and later, J. Vin D'Cruz and William Steele (2000). NSM enables emotion terminologies in the Iban language to be explicated and further defined along the Concrete/Abstract Cultural Continuum framework. By employing these two analytical tools, the readers are then able to see and understand what is truly happening in the mind of the Ibans.

On the presentation of this book, Chapter 1 introduces the readers to the statement of the problem—that the Ibans tend to express their emotions in non-verbal forms, and are therefore, prone to misinterpretation by the culturally insensitive. A clarification of core concepts relevant to the research (e.g. culture, values, communication, etc.) is also included in this chapter. Chapter 2 outlines the specific cultural and structural aspects of the Ibans' way of life, including the communal life of the longhouse, their religion, the law of *adat*, the earlier practice of headhunting in the ancient times, their language and the Ibans' relationship to the spiritual world, the society and the nature. Chapter 3 explains the methodology used for analysis and discussions of the emotion concepts in this ethic group, with particular reference to Natural Semantic Metalanguage and the Concrete/Abstract Cultural Continuum framework. The data were gathered through interviews and my own personal observation of the selected Iban speakers. The respondents of this study were the villagers from Sbangki Panjai, which is an Iban longhouse located in Lubok Antu, Sarawak (i.e. one of the states in Malaysia). Needless to say, as an Iban speaker myself and also one of the longhouse members, I encountered no restrictions in interacting with the respondents while conducting this research. Chapter 4 presents the explications and discussions of the Iban emotion concepts, which include the findings and analyses of interview results and observations. Finally, Chapter 5 summarises the findings, draws out some significant implications, highlights the limitations of the study and suggests recommendations for further research in the area.

The findings of this research significantly reveal the core cultural values that underlie the behavioural conduct of the Ibans in the ways they express their emotional feelings. The concept of *adat* and the rules of speaking in this ethnic community, in particular, are discussed in detail in this book, which explain the communicative behaviours of these people. This book offers insights into the Ibans' world of meanings that essentially describes how these people relate themselves to others in their interaction.

Lilly Metom
February 2013

ACKNOWLEDGEMENTS

I am profoundly grateful to my former employer, Universiti Malaysia Sabah, for sponsoring me to undertake my master's degree and attending to my financial needs throughout the length of my studies. I am indebted to the late Professor Vin D'Cruz, my supervisor, who first introduced me to the area of Language and Culture. I am also deeply grateful to Dr. Subakir and Dr. Hazidi for reading and commenting on my thesis. My gratification also goes to Amy, Saira, Lydia, Maureen, Affidah, Huzai, Aiza and Norlida for being supportive friends. I'm also truly grateful to Jones Mackean, a good friend of mine, who has generously granted the permission to use his splendid pictures, especially the one on the cover page. Special thanks go to my family, my mom and dad, my brothers and sister, Ramzi, Bobby, Robenson and Sophia, for their endless moral support, love and encouragement. Thanks also go to my brother-in-law, Balachandran, who has given his encouragement and moral support to this book publication. Last but not least, I am deeply indebted to my husband, Thony, for his valuable love, care and support, and my three lovely sons, Joel, Ashley and Daniell, who are the apples of my eyes.

LIST OF TABLES

LIST OF FIGURES

CHAPTER 1

INTRODUCTION

Introduction

What makes human beings unique and distinguished from other animals is that—we possess a language system that allows us to interact and communicate with one another. We use the language that we know to interact with different people for multiple purposes, such as playing, fighting, discussing, negotiating, and so forth. In fact, there is hardly a moment in our lives that is free from interaction. It is language that serves as the source of human life and power (Fromkin & Rodman, 1993). Sapir (1961, p.46) argues that,

> "[n]o tribe has ever been found which is without language, and all statements to the contrary may be dismissed as mere folklore. There seems to be no warrant whatever for the statements which is sometimes made that there are certain people whose vocabulary is so limited that they cannot get on without the supplementary use of gesture so that intelligible communication between members of such a group becomes impossible in the dark. The truth of the matter is that language is an essentially perfect means of expression and communication among every known people. Of all aspects of culture, it is fair guess that language was the first to receive a highly developed form and that its essential perfection is a prerequisite to the development of culture as a whole."

Furthermore, Sapir (1961, p.46) also states that every known group of human beings is characterized by "a gift of speech and a well ordered language." Language is viewed as a perfect system of symbols for expressing meanings in any culture that serves as an essential means of expression, which in a way is a great force of human socialization.

We may not know how language exactly originated, however, we do know that language is an essential tool of communication, such as to express emotions. As pointed out by Otto Jespersen (1921, in Yule, 1993), human language originated while humans were actually enjoying themselves. Although Jespersen's suggestion is speculative, it does make sense to say that language serves as a crucial human's tool for expressing meanings to others. Moreover, to say that language is a great force for human socialization is to signify that it does not only function as a tool for allowing social interaction, but also as a powerful source of a common speech which serves as "a peculiarly potent symbol of the social solidarity" of those who speak the language (Sapir, 1961, p. 52).

In addition, Wierzbicka (1992, p.373) states that, "language is a mirror of culture". There is indeed a strong relationship between language and culture. Undoubtedly, different cultures express feelings or emotions in different ways. The Iban people, for instance, who are the subject of this research, have their unique style in expressing emotions. The expressions of emotion words are often converted using non-verbal acts, in which the people understand one another clearly even though there is no involvement of verbal utterances. Furthermore, Howell (1909) describes the Ibans as reserved when it comes to emotional expressions. Most Ibans prefer to reserve their emotional thoughts instead of conveying their feelings into explicit verbal utterances. However, there are times when the Ibans resort to borrowing from other languages, especially Malay, in their attempt to express their emotions to others. In fact, nowadays, borrowing has become an important means to express emotions in Iban culture in addition to non-verbal expressions.[1] Why then does the Iban language borrow from

---

[1]   Chapter 4 will describe in detail the subject of borrowing and how the Ibans express their emotions using non-verbal gestures.

other languages? Aren't there words in Iban that fit the description of the said emotions?

Hence, this research study intends to investigate and analyse how the concepts of emotions are expressed in the Iban community in Sarawak.

Statement of the Problem

Different cultures speak in different ways in countries all over the world. This difference involves the diverse use of linguistic codes, which include the different uses of lexicons and grammar, as well as different ways of using the codes (Wierzbicka, 1991). Theories of speech acts and conversational logic have tended to assume that the ways of speaking characteristic of mainstream white American English represent the normal human ways of speaking; however, these theories turn out to be an ethnocentric illusion. Many studies have been carried out in the attempt to search for universality in language usage utilizing the culture-specific explanation. Brown and Levinson's (1987, in Wierzbicka, 1991) principles of 'politeness phenomena' is one amongst them. Recent studies have shown that the basic conceptual tools introduced and relied on by the researchers (the notion of 'face' in particular) have in fact a strong Anglo-centric bias. Brown and Levinson see two principles as the most important ones in human interaction—they are avoidance of imposition (i.e. 'negative face') and approval of the other person. The same charge of anglocentrism can be made to various other supposedly universal maxims and principles of human conversational behavioural and interaction. For example, Leech's (1983, in Wierzbicka, 1991) maxim of 'modesty' indicates that one minimizes dispraise of other and maximizes praise of other, while Leech's maxim of approbation points out that one minimizes praise of self and maximizes praise of self. Empirical evidence suggests that the maxims are not universally valid. For example, Kochman (1981, in Wierzbicka, 1991) has shown that in Black American culture, the norm of 'modesty' does not apply, and that self-praise is not viewed negatively at all. Likewise, Mitzumi-Mitzumi (1987, in Wierzbicka, 1991) shows that 'approbation' or 'praise of other' is not encouraged in the Japanese culture. Similarly, Honna-Hoffer (1989, in Wierzbicka, 1991) points out that 'praise of other' is seen as arrogant and presumptuous in the Japanese culture. Thus, it is not true that all human societies view 'praise of self' negatively, and 'praise of other' positively.

Language studies associated with the term 'cross-cultural pragmatics' reveal that different speech communities have their own unique ways of interacting. These ways of communication are organized and meaningful which reflect diverse cultural values of the communities. Furthermore, these diverse means of interacting can be described in accordance with "independently established different cultural values and cultural priorities" (Wierzbicka, 1991, p.68).

Cultures differ in their styles of communication as exemplified by the Black American and Japanese cultures mentioned earlier, and the Iban culture is no exception. The Ibans' style of interaction is also unique, in which expressions of emotions in Iban cannot be simply explained or translated into English since meanings and utilization of the expressions are culture specific. Moreover, based on the fact that the Iban people are more concrete[2] in their relation with other members of the group, expressions of emotions, such as anger, sadness, joy, fear and others, are normally conveyed non-verbally. There are no words in the Iban language for 'sorry' or even 'thank you'. What are the equivalences of these emotion terminologies in Iban then? Does the Iban language borrow from other languages (e.g. Malay) in order to provide for the missing words? If it does, why is it so?

Thus, this research (as noted earlier) explores how emotions are expressed by the Ibans, particularly how they are conveyed and utilized in the daily conducts of this ethnic group. In order to explain culturally the emotion words, natural semantic metalanguage (NSM)[3] is used as an

---

[2] Detailed discussions on the concreteness of the Ibans are included in Chapter 4; meanwhile, the notions of concreteness and abstraction will be further defined in Chapter 3.

[3] The subject of Natural Semantic Metalanguage will be explained in detail in Chapter 3.

analytical tool to explicate the emotion words, so as to avoid ethnocentric bias.

Research Questions

This research intends to seek answers to several questions raised in relation to the Iban concepts of emotional expressions. The following are the three major research questions of this study:

1. How do the Iban people convey their emotional thoughts?
2. In relation to their way of interaction, where is the Ibans' location on the concrete/abstract cultural continuum?
3. Do the Ibans borrow from other languages in their attempt to convey their emotions?

Significance of the Study

It is important for us to understand how cultures differ in their ways of interaction. With regard to the concepts of emotion, the Iban people have their own unique ways in conveying their different emotions (e.g. joy, anger, gratitude, affection, surprise, fear, etc.). Wierzbicka (1991, 1992) remarks more generally that such concepts of emotion cannot be simply explained using English words, for otherwise, the explanation will be imposed by ethnocentric bias. By studying the emotion concepts of the Iban culture, we would be able to study the unique cultural perceptions of the people and how they perceive their world around them. In addition, we are also in the position to assess elements of concreteness reflected in the ways the Ibans express their emotions. Hence, it becomes possible to make a comparative study of the interactional styles of the Ibans and other speech communities, such as the Malays. Finally, we could also draw conclusions as to why the Ibans borrow from other languages (i.e. Malay and English) in their attempt to express their emotions.

Clarifying Some Relevant Concepts

In order to understand the matters discussed in this research study, a clear understanding of some relevant concepts is essentially required. The definitions and clarifications provided here will help the reader understand the important and relevant concepts used in the discussions. The following sections will describe and clarify several related terms and concepts.

Culture

There are many definitions of culture as offered by various researchers, such as Taylor (1958), Kluckhom (1949), Hofstede (1994), and Parsons and Kroeber (1958). However, Asma (1996) summarizes all the definitions given by the researchers and offers a compressed and synthesized definition of the term. According to Asma (1996, p.4), culture refers to,

- "the total patterns of beliefs, customs, practices, institutions, techniques and objects that people of a society have invented, adopted and inherited from their forefathers other reliable sources.
- an integrated and shared pattern of human behaviour that includes thought, speech, action and artefacts, and its survival depends on the capacity of the members to learn and transmit knowledge to succeeding generations so that they know how they are expected to behave.
- a way of life which gives members in a society a sense of purpose, identity, meaning and well-being and generates a commitment to the primary cultural values and philosophy—the vision that members believe they can promote and uphold.
- the cumulative deposit of knowledge, experience, meanings, beliefs, values, attitudes and concepts of self, the universe (reality, harmony with nature and hierarchies of status), time, role expectations and spatial relations acquired by a large group of people in the course of generations through individuals and groups striving in order to adapt to the environment."

Thus, culture is essential to every society or community in the world. It refers to a way of life of the members of society, or groups of people within a society. This way of life consists of how we as members of the community perceive and interpret the world around us by means of relating our ideas and beliefs, and how we relate with other people and organize our daily conduct of life. Culture shapes and forges individuals as communicators, and it also constructs our individual social realities and repertoires of communicative behaviours and meanings.

People view their world based on categories, concepts and labels of their culture. When one culture coincides with another, sharing becomes possible in intercultural communication. Our ways of communicating, our communicative circumstances, our language styles, as well as our non-verbal behaviours are primarily based on our cultural knowledge and values that we very much try to preserve (Asma, 1996; Porter & Samovar, 1991).

Values

In a general sense, values are the major key of understanding the detailed meaning of culture. They are the mental orientation or underlying assumptions which members of the group understand and share with one other. In addition, they include the invisible aspects of culture, which at times can only be observed by looking at one's behaviours. Hence, values are the central element of a culture that serves as our guidelines to proper daily behavioural conducts. They determine the belief system of a group—that is, they define the subjects or elements which are worthy of protection and sacrifice. This belief system also clarifies what are considered to be proper subjects for study and ridicule, and what is worth preserving in order to maintain group solidarity. They also inform the group members of what is good and bad, right and wrong, true and false, positive and negative, and so forth (Asma, 1996).

Values provide an individual or a society with the wisdom to live, that is by presenting them with the rationale and logic to conduct their daily activities. They serve as important frameworks of preference. Based on these frameworks, members of the group assess their judgement, behaviours and emotions. In other words, values mirror the cultural norms that govern the rules in a society. By adhering to these underlying assumptions, society members relate themselves with the world around them (Asma, 1996; Porter & Samovar, 1991). Moreover, Asma (1996, p.12) further elaborates that,

> "members of a group develop a set of beliefs and convictions about how the world actually is, attitudes which are predispositions to perform, perceive, ideas, feeling and specific opinions which are concrete expressions of particular issues."

Asma (1996, p.12) also mentions that cultural values are "a set of clear and uncompromising statements" which detail the significant elements to the group members. These values become the guide to the members' individual behaviours that offer meaning and function as social bonds for the ethnic group. They are customarily performed and displayed by means of some form of mutual rites that are often practised by members of the family and significant elders of the community. Asma (1996, p.13) indicates that "our culture provides standards that permit us to make decisions about our relationships with ourselves, our friends, other members of the society, Nature and God."

Communication

The knowledge of human communication is crucial for understanding cross-cultural interaction. This is because, it enables us to investigate what happens during communicative encounters, the reasons and effects of the communicative events, as well as the things people do to influence and heighten the outcomes of human communication. Communication becomes the means of where we establish social links with other people.

The behaviours that we generate, either spoken or unspoken, or either intentionally or unintentionally (e.g. talking, smiling, laughing, running, frowning, shaking our head, etc.) are referred to as *messages* that will elicit responses from other people. The response to the observed behaviour relies on the responder's knowledge, experience and social context. Porter and Samovar (1991, p.8) define communication as "a dynamic transactional behaviour-affecting process in which people behave intentionally in order to induce or elicit a particular response from another person." The researchers argue that communication is complete only when the intended message is received by the intended recipient, and he or she reacts to and is influenced by the communicative message. For these to occur, the transactions must comprise all oblivious, intentional or unintentional, spoken or unspoken, and contextual stimuli that serve as signals about the quality and integrity of the messages. Thus, communication is a continuous and dynamic activity, which is interactive and irreversible in attribute.

Aims of the Study

The following are the aims of the study:

1. To explicate the Iban emotion concepts using Natural Semantic Metalanguage (NSM)
2. To locate the Ibans' interactional style on the abstract/concrete cultural continuum
3. To find out the loanwords usage in the Iban emotion concepts

Limitations of the Study

Many publications have been produced in the areas of emotions and Natural Semantic Metalanguage (NSM). However, with regard to the Iban emotion concepts, there has been no study carried out on this subject to the best of my knowledge while doing this research and reading on the area. In fact, most research studies on the Ibans have focused on the community's way of life, such as the religion, migration, headhunting rites, festivals, paddy cultivation, and so forth. Therefore, the evaluation and explication of the Iban emotion concepts utilizing NSM in this research are based on my own perceptions and knowledge as a member of the ethnic group.

It is noted that the selected group of the Ibans in this study does not represent the whole population of this ethnic community in Sarawak. There are many dialects of the Iban language found in Sarawak, namely, the Simanggang dialect, Saratok dialect, Sibu dialect, Miri dialect, and so forth. These different dialects may have their different ways of expressing their emotion concepts. Hence, this study is limited to the selected group comprising the Iban speakers at Sbangki Panjai Longhouse, Lubok Antu.

CHAPTER II
LITERATURE REVIEW

Introduction

As far as this research is concerned, no studies have been done on the concepts of emotions in relation to the Iban culture. However, the Iban emotion concepts can be discussed by looking at the Malay culture, since both cultures express their emotion concepts almost in similar patterns (e.g. anger—*marah*, and shame—*malu*). In fact, it is evident that the Ibans tend to borrow from the Malay language when it comes to emotional expressions in certain aspects of emotion speech.

Several authors, such as Wazir (1990), Wierzbicka (1991, 1992), Abu-Lughod and Lutz (1990), as well as Goddard (1997, 1998), have discussed the universal concepts of emotions. In relation to language attitudes and identities, Mohamad Subakir (1998) provides useful insights in his study on the changing patterns of communication and language use among the Javanese community in Sungai Lang, Malaysia. According to Mohamad Subakir (1998), language provides a rich means of expressing social identity in human cultures. Writing extensively on his subject matter, the author discovers the process of language shift from Javanese to Malay that is taking place in the Javanese community, which, as he argues, is evidence of language loss. From his study, Mohamad Subakir (1998) also reveals that the people have negative attitudes towards Javanese to the extent of viewing the language as a handicap to the development of children's education and socio-economic advancement. In addition, they tend to associate Javanese with the lifestyle of the uneducated, rural, 'peasant' people. On the contrary, the Javanese in the community bear positive attitudes towards Malay, associating the language with the lifestyle of the urban and values of pan-Malaysians. They consider the Malay language as more useful and prestigious than Javanese.

As will be discussed in the following sections of this chapter, it is also important for us to include some background knowledge of the Iban people and their culture, as well as those values which are of great importance to the ethnic group. Several authors, such as Asmah (1981), Sutlive (1994), Richards (1981), Howell (1908, 1909, 1910), Sandin (1967, 1980) Kedit (1980), and Lim (1989), have contributed comprehensively to the study of this indigenous people, resulting in several publications.

Concepts of Emotions across Cultures

Wazir (1990, p.1) defines *emotion* as

"a phenomenon relating to the psychological responses and reactions which individuals display in the course of living together under one cultural system and society, to be distinguished from 'social ethos' or 'social sentiment' which sums up, on a higher level, the constellation of values, norms, and morality upheld by a group of people, produced from the experiences of practising culture in a given society."

This explains that emotions are cultural relics that epitomize mutual understandings of human nature and social communication. In addition, emotions are perceived as ""things" with which social systems must "deal" in a functional sense . . . . and are sometimes treated as psychic "energies" implicitly marshalled in the service of constructing a social order" (Abu-Lughod & Lutz, 1990, p.3).

The concept of emotions also reflects the culture of its speakers. In other words, it embodies a unique way of observing and thinking about the world. However, emotion concepts are not to be simply translated into English. This is because, they reflect different cultural values of the speakers which can only be clarified and understood following diverse cultural values and cultural priorities that have been independently set up in the societies or communities (Wierzbicka, 1992).

In past decades, some scholars claimed that the fundamental human emotions can be possibly identified which are universal, distinct and presumably intrinsic. Izard and Buechler (1980, in Wierzbicka, 1992) indicate that these fundamental emotions are: (1) interest, (2) joy, (3) surprise, (4) sadness, (5) anger, (6) disgust, (7) contempt, (8) fear, (9) shame/shyness, and (10) guilt. However, Wierzbicka (1992) questions on how these emotions can be precisely determined using English words if they are presumed to specify human emotions. Giving an example from the Polish culture, Wierzbicka points out that Polish does not have a word equivalent to the English word 'disgust'. In another instance, Gidjingali—an Australian Aboriginal language, does not lexically distinguish 'fear' from 'shame', subsuming that emotional feelings associated with those recognized by the English words 'fear' and 'shame' are categorized in one lexical item. In addition, Wierzbicka (1992, p.119) also argues that the English emotion terminologies are composed of a folk nomenclature and "not an objective, culture-free analytical framework". Thus, lexical words such as 'disgust', 'fear' and 'shame' cannot be merely presupposed as evidence to human concepts or fundamental psychological reliabilities. Often, these words are considered as if they were objective and natural categories which are free from cultural perceptions. Goddard (1998) also comments that ethnocentrism in research concerning emotions is one source of practice which employs complex and specific terms of English as if they were a universal metalanguage with a culture-free attribute.

Some Features of the Ibans' Lived Culture

The Iban population in Malaysia is one of the huge majorities in the country. Traditionally, these indigenous people are riverine settlers who reside in longhouses situated along major rivers and smaller streams in the rural areas of Sarawak. Energized with vigorous spirit and mobility, the people had dispersed during the last two centuries from the river systems of Batang Lupar and Saribas of Sarawak. From there, they moved from the connecting Kapuas region of western Kalimantan via the heart of Rejang Valley and travelled northward and eastward. Today, they are present in all divisions of Sarawak, settling in both the urban and rural regions; however, the people mainly concentrate in the second and third divisions. The Iban settlements are situated along the banks of major rivers in all the eleven administrative divisions[4] of Sarawak. These rivers are extremely important to the livelihood of the Ibans as they provide them with their water resource and means of transportation (Asmah, 1981; Lim, 1989; Sandin, 1980).

The Ibans are also referred to as the 'Sea Dayaks/Dyaks'. It was Sir James Brooke who gave this designation to the people in the late nineteenth century due to their close relation to the sea. However, nowadays, the term 'Iban' is preferably used in all Sarawak divisions although 'Sea Dayak/ Dyak' is still favoured in the second division (Sandin, 1967). It is also believed that the word 'Iban' originates from the Kayan[5] word *ivan*, which means 'immigrant' or 'wanderer' (Sandin, 1967; Asmah, 1981).

Furthermore, the Ibans are considered as Proto-Malays due to their close resemblance to the Malays in terms of language and physical manifestations. This means that, this ethnic tribe is also grouped in the

---

4   There are eleven administrative divisions in Sarawak, namely, Betong Division, Bintulu Division, Kapit Division, Kuching Division, Limbang Division, Miri Division, Mukah Division, Samarahan Division, Sarikei Division, Sibu Division, and Sri Aman Division.

5   The Kayan tribe is one of the ethnic groups found in Sarawak. This group profoundly resides in the interior of Sarawak, such as in Miri and Bintulu divisions.

same stock as the 'true' Sumatran Malays and the Peninsular Malays. Notably, the main difference from the latter is on the fact that the Ibans are not influenced by Islam and the Muslim culture (Asmah, 1981; Howell, 1908).

The Iban Longhouse

The Ibans are characterised by their social and collective traits. The longhouse, which is their communal home, reflects these attributes in the people. Basically, an Iban longhouse is a compact village, constructed as a single architectural structure which is home to numerous families (see Figure 6). All the community members are related to one another either by blood or marriage. A single longhouse can be home to 15-50 families (sometimes more). A common corridor called *ruai* runs though its entire length (see Figure 11) that functions as a communal place. The longhouse community gathers here to work and socialize, such as pounding the rice, weaving the *pua kumbu* (a kind of Iban rag), basket or mat, chatting and gossiping, or simply babysitting the young ones. During festivals, namely, *Gawai Dayak*, *Gawai Antu* and *Gawai Kenyalang*, the *ruai* serves as a large place for entertainment, such as dancing and drinking of *tuak* (the Iban rice wine). The *ruai* is also used as a communal hall for organizing religious ceremonies (see Figure 12) and discussing serious matters pertaining to the whole community (see Figure 13) (Freeman, 1970; Lim, 1989).

Each longhouse has a head called *tuai rumah*, who is responsible in administering the well-being of the community under his supervision. He is also the arbitrator in issues with regard to spiritual rites and social justice. As the head of the longhouse community, he is accountable to the *penghulu*—the local district leader of the Ibans who serves as the leader of several longhouses in his administrative territory (Freeman, 1970; Lim, 1989). It is expected of the *tuai rumah* to be knowledgeable of the Iban *adat* (the Iban rules of conduct). Through informal assemblies and legal trials, he is expected to comply with the Iban *adat* and resolve disputes that occur within the community.

Since the conciliation of the Ibans and the establishment of European government, the position of *tuai rumah* has gone through numerous changes. Nowadays, the *tuai rumah* also serves as a conciliator between his longhouse and the administrative system, in which the government appoints him as the community representative. He is also responsible for executing the government policies (Freeman, 1970).

In former times, the position of the *tuai rumah* was much less significant as compared to the present. Despite the occurrence of modern changes, there are still limitations in his administrative power within the longhouse community. Notably, the appointment of the *tuai rumah* is not inherited. When the *tuai rumah* dies, his successor is chosen by the longhouse community as a whole. There is, however, no system of voting in selecting the *tuai rumah*. Instead, a general meeting called *baum* will be held at which all men and women of the longhouse express their opinions of whom they favour. Nevertheless, the key feature that determines the appointment of this community head is his kinship affiliation. The longhouse community will likely select the person within the core-group of the closely related as the successor. Besides, the person's personal qualities are also taken into consideration when deciding a *tuai rumah*. Ideally, a *tuai rumah* is a man of good appearance and reputation, and who has accomplished prestige in his community. He should possess the quality of autonomy and the ability to resolve problems, which are the requirements of any leader. Nevertheless, the most important of all, he should be knowledgeable of the Iban *adat*, impartial, well-versed in giving his speeches, and possesses sound judgement in handling communal argument (Freeman, 1970).

Each Iban family has their own separate private apartment called *bilik* for cooking, eating, sleeping and other multitude of domestic tasks (see Figure 8 and Figure 9). It is a common sight to see an opening in the form of a window or a small passage on the side-wall of a *bilik* if the neighbouring families are closely related (see Figure 10). The opening is to provide inter-communication between the family members of the adjoining apartments. The *bilik* is also used for keeping valued properties, for example, *ilang, bebendai, tawak, tajau* (see Figure 14), *pua kumbu,* and other family heirlooms, which will be handed down to succeeding generations. In addition, these units of *biliks* run parallel to the *ruai* (see Figure 11) and open onto it (Freeman, 1970). After the *ruai* is the veranda or walkway called *tanju* (see Figure 7), which is a wide open space on which the paddy is fanned immediately after harvest and put to dry under the direct sun before being stored.

Religion

In religious matters, a large number of the Ibans today have converted to Christianity; however, some still uphold their traditional beliefs, especially those in the interior divisions of Sarawak. Based on the belief in plurality of deities, the old Iban traditions entail the people to pay reverence to gods and goddesses of the Iban mythology (Asmah, 1981). Moreover, writing at the beginning of the twentieth century, Howell (1909, p.17) describes the Iban religion as "a combination of superstitions, complicated and indefinite." The deities or gods, called *petara*, are believed to be "corporeal, possessing bodies and souls, as well as begetting sons and daughters" (Howell, 1909, p.24). Among the principal deities or gods of the Ibans are *Bunsu Ribut*—the god of the wind, *Petara Kebong Langit*—the god of the heavens, *Petara Puchok Kayu*—the god of the trees, and *Petara Tengah Tanah*—the god of the earth (Howell, 1908; Kedit, 1980). The three most significant gods which epitomize the corpus of Iban cultural values and traditions are *Selampandai*—the creator of man, *Singalang Burong*—the god of war, and *Sempulang Gana*—the principal god of the paddy cult. Among all the deities, *Singalang Burung* is the most important god, being both the god of war and the god of universal surveillance of the Iban well-being. In accordance with the Iban mythology, it was *Singalang Burung* who disclosed the secret of rice farming to the Ibans and taught them how to seek the gods' advice. Furthermore, as the god of war, he was summoned to attend ritual ceremonies associated with headhunting during the ancient times. During the headhunting rites, *sampi* (prayers) were uttered, while fowl and pigs were slaughtered for sacrificial offerings to his reverence (Kedit, 1980).

The Iban *Adat*

According to Howell (1908, p.16),

"the Sea Dyaks have their own rules of logic in their courts of law, which are more approximate to axioms than proverbs. To listen to an advocate defending their cases is certainly worth the while if one is conversant with the classical language. They are a political race, more so than the Malays or Chinese. With them all offences are finable. Apologies are not accepted in their society in accordance with their custom."

Most Ibans today still remain as strong, concrete longhouse communities. As members of this indigenous group, despite modernity, the Ibans in the longhouses are still highly confined and constrained by the complex 'rules of logic' called *adat*. Sandin (1980, p.xi) states that,

". . . the term *adat* covers all of the various customary norms, jural rules, ritual interdictions and injunctions that guide an individual's conduct, and the sanctions and forms of redress by which these norms and rules are upheld."

The Iban *adat* functions to assure harmonious relationships among the community. For the Ibans, *adat* applies to all aspects of their lives, namely, in social matters, economics, religion and politics. It is important to stress that the Iban *adat* is somehow in contrast to the Malay *adat*. Notably, in the Iban community, there is no distinction between *adat* and religious canons and practices. In fact, many of the elements in the Iban *adat* originate from religious beliefs and exist due to concerns of ritual observances and other aspects of the Iban existence. In addition, the Iban *adat* is also not confined to the customary law, whereby several constituents of the *adat* are imposed by the constitution of legal means, especially authorized by fines. Sandin (1980, p.xii) points out that, "*adat* also regulates interpersonal relationships and defines the respective rights and responsibilities of individuals standing in different relationships to another. It also stipulates the rights persons may enjoy in land and other tangible property and the manner in which these rights may be inherited or otherwise transferred from one person or group to another."

Adat also comprises the personal behaviours of the Ibans, which is similar to the English concept of custom. In relation to this, a person's behavioural manner can be expressed as having either good or bad *adat*. Sandin (1980) mentions that a person with good *adat* does not only entail that the behaviour of the person adheres to the exact rules of *adat* as already acknowledged in his or her community, it also reveals the abstract qualities of the person, for instance, the person's generosity or personal courage. Thus, *adat* is a code for personal conduct in an individual, which is expected of the individual in his or her relationship with others. A person with good *adat* is seen as well-mannered, verbally courteous, respectful, and sincere towards other people in his or her interaction with them. In addition, good *adat* also signifies good breeding in an individual and a dignified social control in one's physical and non-verbal behaviours. Hence, the Ibans see the notion of *adat* as rules that govern more common values, ethics and principles. Besides, *adat* also functions as the essential measure or gauge against which the individual's behaviour can be evaluated and judged.

Sandin (1980) further emphasizes that *adat* has strong normative attributes, in which the rules in *adat* determine the things or matters that should or should not be carried out in various situations. *Adat* directs an individual to perform correct behaviours and ensures the maintenance of moral order as well as the continued existence of the Iban society itself. When *adat* is violated, it is described as *penyalah*—glossed as 'wrongful act' in bilingual dictionaries. Wrongful acts, which are those acts that contradict the Iban *adat*, will induce displeasure among the community, and in many circumstances, will be judged which will result in the individual paying some form of fine. Sandin (1980, p.xiii) asserts that, "when the Ibans discuss *adat* they often use the term to describe, in any given situation, both the rules of behaviour that apply and also the correct punishment to be meted out should these rules be transgressed. The term *adat* applies to both. For many transgressions, punishment takes the form of fines, or reparations of value. The notion of fines (*tunggu*) is closely associated with *adat* and written codifications of *adat* are characteristically described as *tusun tunggu*, or "fine lists" . . . Traditionally, *tunggu* is a reparation payable to the injured party and mutually agreed to by both disputants. This is distinguished from the more recent *ukum*, an imposed fine or penalty, retained all or in part by the government or presiding authority."

However, after the Brookes arrived in Sarawak in 1842, the Iban fines underwent systemization whereby monetary equivalents were assigned (Sandin, 1980).

Furthermore, when a person causes personal harm or loss of properties to another Iban individual, this is seen as a violation of *adat*. The Ibans view this violation as an assault to the soul or spiritual character of the victim. Hence, in order to revive the victim's soul, the transgressor has to present a ritual redress. Sandin (1980, p.xiv) states that,

"wrongful acts often have spiritual consequences, or are thought to invite the supernatural punishment, and the notions further reinforce the moral authority of *adat*, and the application of fines and more diffuse social sanctions in maintaining compliance."

Adat ultimately governs the personal conduct of every individual in the Iban community. When an individual becomes a victim of a wrongdoing, it is expected of him or her to *minta adat* ('to ask for *adat*'), which means—he or she has the right to ask for a compensation based on the stipulated laws of *adat*. The *tuai rumah* and other community seniors are responsible to ensure that accurate fines and ritual sanctions are executed and every redress act is attended to. This is to ensure that the *adat* is maintained which will eventually result in the restoration of social harmony and spiritual health of the whole Iban community (Sandin, 1980; Freeman, 1970).

Maintaining good moral values in any Iban society is crucially important. This is signified in one of the *adat* rules, which greatly concerns with telling the truths to other people. When this code of conduct is transgressed, the punishment for the dishonourable liar is to pile a *tugong bula* (a liar's heap) in memory of the person. The Iban community deems a lie as one of the most disgraceful offences. When an individual has uttered an immense lie, branches or twigs are heaped on the shoulder of the main road or at a common spot where everyone who passes by will add a branch or stick to it. The logic behind this practice is to remind the future generations of the person's wickedness and take warning from it. The deceived person starts the *tugong bula* by stacking a large number of branches and followed by other contributors. The contribution to the *tugong bula* is perceived as the Ibans' sacred responsibility. Therefore, anyone who fails to do so is believed to invite supernatural catastrophe to his or her being (Anonymous, 1904; Howell, 1910). Moreover, the branches are not only piled by the contributors, but they will also add words of curse to the heap in memory of the condemned cheater. Starting from a few branches of twigs, the liar's heap will eventually grow in size. Once the pile gets too big, it will be torched to ashes. Later, another new *tugong bula* is heaped to substitute the former one, and the process continues and repeats. The liar's heap becomes a testimony to the person's untruthfulness for succeeding generations to witness. To an Iban, it is a standing disgrace to the liar's generations. Furthermore, the condemned liar is not the only person who suffers the disgrace, his or her later generations who are not yet born will also have to put up with the shame (Anonymous, 1904; Howell, 1910). Hence, a family's reputation suffers from the misdeeds of its past member. For this reason, *adat* is of special importance to the Ibans. It does not only safeguard the social harmony among the longhouse community, but also ensures possible ritual collaboration upon which their communal interests and welfare are thought to rely on.

Headhunting

Headhunting has long been a popular topic of interest in relation to the Ibans of Sarawak. The people were known for their so-called aggressive headhunting tradition in the past. Before the British arrived in Sarawak, the Iban culture was governed by the heroic code of the warrior. The status and prestige of the indigenous tribe were determined by its capability in warfare, demonstrated through the acquisition of the number of human heads captured in battles with other tribal groups (Lim, 1989). It was the headhunting practice in the old Iban tradition in the past that has given Sarawak this appellation—the 'Land of the Headhunters'.

There were several reasons attributed to the headhunting practice in Sarawak in the ancient times. Firstly, it indicated the end of grieving period for the deceased. When there was a bereavement in the longhouse, the grieving period could only be ended by procuring a fresh human head. This rite was believed to keep the victim's soul, as well as to infuse new energy and life into the community (Lim, 1989; Metcalf, 1996). Secondly, headhunting also attested the courage of a man in the Iban society. Warriors who returned with the enemies' heads after a successful *kayau* (closely translated as 'raid') were ceremoniously celebrated as a recognition of their bravery and triumph for bringing back the 'trophies' (i.e. the heads of the enemies). In the ancient Iban traditions, the human head was perceived as the most precious of all possessions as it symbolized bravery and power. Thirdly, the headhunting practice was carried out as a form of revenge for crimes (e.g. murder and theft) committed by one tribe against another. For instance, whenever a person became a murder victim of another tribe, a *kayau* expedition would soon be declared (Gomez, 2004). Finally, in the old customs of Iban marriage ritual, the bride's father would demand an enemy's head as a dowry from the bridegroom. The taking of the human head was viewed as the man's proof of bravery in slaying his enemy (Asmah, 1981; Gomez, 2004). Nevertheless, all these ancient customs pertaining to headhunting are no longer observed in these modern days.

James Brooke or Rajah Brooke, the British sea-adventurer who founded a dynasty of three generations in Sarawak, finally illegalized the practice of headhunting after the Second World War. It was Rajah Brooke who eventually brought to an end the savage and adventurous spirits of the Ibans. However, to date, reminders of the ancient days can still be seen in many Iban longhouses. In fact, most of these longhouse communities are still proud of their enemies' skulls which hang down from the ceiling of their *ruai* or corridor (Asmah, 1981; Lim, 1989).

Language

The Iban language is spoken by about a third of Sarawak population. It is also the language conversed in varying dialects by the Iban tribes or the closely related 'Ibanic' peoples of Kalimantan, who dwell in the north bank of the Kapuas River. Within Sarawak, the language is used as a lingua franca wherever the people have settled. Being one of the majorities in the state, Iban becomes a major means of interacting between the people and other races (Richards, 1981; Sutlive, 1994).

In terms of vocabulary items, numerous lexical words have been added into the language due to the people's contact with other ethnic groups. Various words have been adopted which enrich the Iban vocabulary (Howell, 1908). It is also believed that most loanwords in Iban have entered the language through Malay. It is noted that the Malay language has also borrowed many words from Sanskrit during the Majapahit rule (Asmah, 1981). Nevertheless, it is hard to ascertain as to which of the two languages (i.e. Malay and Iban) is the richer and more expressive. However, according to Howell (1908), both languages are highly expressive and remarkably melodious when they are grammatically verbalized.

Iban is grouped in the Western Austronesian family; however, it is not readily intelligible to a speaker of the Peninsular or Indonesian Malays. Despite its distinctive features from the Malay language, it has a close relation to it. Asmah (1981, p.5) states that,

> "[t]he existence of certain structural as well as lexical affinities between the two languages has led several authors to treat Iban as a dialect of Malay."

Even though Iban is closely related to Malay and the fact that it shares a large number of lexical words with the language (i.e. Malay), the two languages are not mutually intelligible. Notably, about 60 per cent of the basic words in Iban and Malay are cognates.

Iban is homogeneous, whereby there are only a few dialect words. Regardless of the dispersion of the Ibans over various regions in Sarawak and other parts of the Peninsular Malaysia, the language is characterized by its astonishing homogeneity. This may be due to their relatively quite recent settlement in western Borneo and frequent contact between the diverse Iban groups. Nevertheless, differences between the Iban speakers of the settlement areas are mostly in the accent, as well as the details in customs and rites. However, the extremes are the Saribas Ibans of the northern second division, who have assimilated with the earlier residents and are closely associated with the Malays. They were the first to profit from the literacy opportunities administered by mission schools. On the other hand, the pioneer Iban communities are those who have settled in Ulu Ai and Baleh, located on the eastern region of Sarawak. Other Iban speakers are mainly identified based on the names of the rivers of Sarawak second division. Seemingly, there is no problem of intelligibility among these Iban groups in understanding one another during communicative encounters (Asmah, 1981; Richards, 1981).

The Iban language does not have its own writing system. However, it has adopted the Latin alphabet via the Christian missionaries' efforts. Furthermore, because the written tradition was nonexistent, the Iban literature comprised entirely of oral narrations. It was Borneo Literature Bureau in Kuching which began to convert the oral literature into its written form. On the other hand, unlike Malay, there are no phonemes in the Iban language, which are peculiar to borrowed words. This is also the same with loan-affixes, even though as far as loanwords (from Sanskrit, Arabic, English, etc.) are concerned, they are adopted into the Iban language via Malay (Asmah, 1981).

With regard to the role of Iban in the education system, it is one of the subjects taught in Sarawak primary and secondary schools. At present, the Iban language is taught up to Form Five.

Relationships of the Ibans with 'Others'

As shown in Figure 1, there are three forms of relationship of the Ibans with the particular 'Others', namely; the Ibans with the Spiritual World, the Ibans with Society, and the Ibans with Nature. The self in the Ibans is being influenced by these elements of 'Others' (i.e. Spiritual World, Society and Nature) that surround their daily lives.

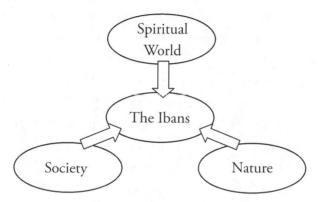

Figure 1: The relationships of the Ibans and 'Others'

The Ibans and the Spiritual World

The Iban religion is based on a belief in the spirits of human, nature and super-nature. They have a strong tendency to relate themselves directly to their deities, in which the revelation of the deities or gods is communicated through dreams or visions. The Ibans regard dreams as oracles from the gods (Kedit, 1980).

The people express the connection and interdependence of their social organization, agricultural practice and religion to the order revealed by their gods. As mentioned earlier, according to the Iban mythology, *Singalang Burung* was the deity who introduced the Ibans to the secret of rice farming and taught them how to seek for gods' advice. As he was also the god of war, the Ibans invoked *Singalang Burung* to attend ritual ceremonies that were connected with the headhunting rite.

The Ibans' direct relationship with their gods is displayed in the practice and preservation of *adat*. In a traditional Iban society, ritual and spiritual beliefs play an important role in upholding the *adat*. Large areas of *adat* are believed to have been revealed or bestowed upon their beings by the gods. Therefore, if *adat* is defied, it is believed to invite divine discontentment and plausible retribution by the gods and spirits. Although the retribution may occur to the transgressor alone, very often it is also believed to menace the whole community to which the transgressor belongs. Hence, violation of *adat* by any individual is believed to bring his or her community into spiritual peril. In the ancient times, such offender would be ostracized by his or her communal members if the transgression was a severe case (Sandin, 1980; Freeman, 1970).

Wrongful acts bear supernatural repercussions in the Iban culture. They are thought to upset the relation of the Ibans with their spiritual world, and therefore, necessitate ritual propositions. The Ibans believe that failure to repair the wrongdoings by ritual means will incite supernatural retaliation which will threaten the harmony of the whole community. Thus, for grave offences, such as incest, the community to which the transgressor belongs to is believed to be under the danger of supernatural peril. In such cases, the offender has to carry out a ritual reparation in order to ensure the collective well-being of the community.

The maintenance of *adat* implies that any individual's action will create a collective consequence to others especially when it involves bad deeds. This explains the strong tendency of the Ibans in relating their daily conducts to the tangible others (i.e. those who are immediately around them). In fact, every Iban person becomes a unit in the community whose action will be greatly defined by the *adat* that governs the entire communal living, that is—one's action is deeply affected by the relationship between the self and others which is held together by the culture of the community. In return for one's absolute steadfastness to the Iban *adat,* the community will bestow the individual with a social security, in which he or she will receive social comfort, group reassurance and indefinite harmony.

The Ibans and Society

The Ibans' direct relationship with their community is strong evidence of their concrete culture. In the communal living of this ethnic group, there exists between them a strong attachment of sentiment which provides the community a continuity of living. This strong attachment is also in part the result of broader relationships, which inspire all societal beings in every corner of the world.

There are two categories of relationship in the Iban community. The first relationship, which comprises the family members, is highly important to this ethnic group. This kindred group stitches the members together through a genealogical connection comprising relatives ranging from grandparents to first cousins, together with the husbands and wives of any persons within this range. The second relationship, which refers to kinship ties, also stems from the people's desire of living collectively in a community rather than in segregation. Besides providing the Ibans with personal security, it also enables them to experience enjoyment and human diversities of societal reality. This social inclination directs to certain communal actions which intend to give a sense of unity to the people. It later grows into a comradeship that ties the group members together (Freeman, 1970).

The longhouse structure itself also reflects the value of a collective community in the Iban culture that significantly reinforces and enhances the sense of group solidarity. The *ruai* (i.e. corridor) of a longhouse serves as a communal hall for social activities, such as chatting and gossiping, entertaining, *pua kumbu* weaving, basket and mat platting, woodcarving and others, which signifies a strong sense of concreteness of the Iban culture. The Ibans are social people who find comfort and satisfaction in the communal living. The *ruai* provides them with the space for this societal desire to be with others, in which they seek each other's companionship and relate directly to one another in every aspect of their communal life. Furthermore, the *ruai* also becomes their platform for discussing serious matters. When there are disputes and conflicts in the community, *adat* becomes the crucial guide that governs the judicial demeanours of the disputing or conflicting parties. Bound by the *adat* system, the Ibans are moulded together as one concrete society. The *tuai rumah* (i.e. the head of the longhouse) will then execute his role as the chief custodian of the community *adat*. Moreover, the fact that the Iban *biliks* (i.e. the apartments in the longhouse) are attached to one another also exhibits a strong bond of communal affiliation among the people. Indeed, the longhouse itself provides the people with societal security of communal living (Freeman, 1970; Lim 1989; Jensen, 1974).

The sense of concreteness is also mirrored in the Iban culture of farming. It is important to note that the subsistence economy of the Ibans is based on the cultivation of paddy. With regard to this, the Iban community has a system in paddy farming called *bedurok*. This system involves a collaborative work group on the basis of labour-exchange. This group may toil the farm during all or any of the four main phases of paddy cultivation, which comprise clearing the jungles, planting, weeding and harvesting. This labour-exchange party differs in size that may consist of three to six families. During *bedurok*, it is the responsibility of the family whose farm is being toiled to provide food and beverage of many types to the workers, such as cooked rice, preserved fish, meat, vegetables, *tuak* (rice wine), and so forth (Freeman, 1970). *Bedurok* also becomes a festive ceremony to the Iban community, particularly during the annual planting of the 'sacred rice' (*belaboh padi pun*). After a hard-day work in the farm, the workers will be nourished and entertained with delicacies and drinks prepared by the host family. The event then results in a festivity that cultivates goodwill among those involved (Freeman, 1970). This clearly signifies a strong concrete relationship between the self and the society in the Iban people.

The Ibans and Nature

The Ibans dwell amongst natural surroundings in the ecological systems of tropical rain forests. The community coexists harmoniously with the jungles and the inhabitants, namely, the trees, rivers, animals, and myriads of insects. They share the ecosystem of jungle life with other non-human organisms. The Ibans naturally relate and translate their world in accordance with their surroundings. They perceive life as a constant process of balancing the existence of all beings, both naturally and supernaturally. The people also believe that all objects and creatures posses their own souls. In their daily conducts, human souls and that of deities or gods often impinge on one another. In fact, the Iban cultural values and social norms derive from this belief on the natural and supernatural environments (Kedit, 1980).

In the traditional Iban community, the people view augury as a means of conveying divine messages from gods to human beings (Sandin, 1980). Sandin (1980: xxxi) elaborates,

"augury is based on a belief that the gods reveal their favour, or issue warnings to mankind through the bearers on their behalf. Augury is the most important of several forms of divination practised by the Ibans, including also dream interpretation and hepatoscopy. In addition to the seven principal augural birds, auguries may also be taken, under special circumstances, from the behaviour of other birds, reptiles, animals and insects, or from natural occurrences. The term *burong* which has the primary meaning of bird, is applied more abstractly to auguries generally, either auguries or, by extension, those conveyed by any of these other natural agencies. By far the greatest cultural significance attaches to bird omens however. The seven augural birds are thought to be the earthly manifestations of gods and they alone are made use of in taking deliberate, formal auguries (*beburong*) whenever divine sanction is sought in support of an important human undertaking."

The Ibans are cautiously attentive to the manners of augural birds and other animals which are believed to act as agents for communicating divine messages from the deities or gods. These celestial messages are deemed to bear warnings and directions, or carry prophecies of forthcoming happenings. The flights and calls of the augural birds are of great significance in the Iban culture.

The people associate the bird omens to *Singalang Burong*, who holds the utmost power among all the Ibans' mythological gods. *Singalang Burong* is believed to possess the prime charge over prophetic communication between the deities and mankind. It is also believed that he is responsible in releasing the omen birds to the world of humans. Needless to say, there are seven principal birds of augury in the Iban community as shown in Table 1 below.

Table 1: Seven principal birds of augury in the Iban community

Iban Name	Scientific Name	Common English Name
Ketupong	*Sasia Abnormis*	Rufous Piculet
Embuas	*Lacedo Pulchella*	Branded Kingfisher
Beragai	*Harpactes Duvauceli*	Scarlet-rumped Trogon
Papau or Kalabu	*Harpactes Diardi*	Diard's Trogon
Bejampong	*Platylophus Galericulatus*	Crested Jay
Pangkas	*Blythipious Rubiginosus*	Maroon Woodpecker
Nendak	*Copsychus Malabaricus*	White-rumped Shama

(Sandin, 1980)

These omen birds are believed to reveal themselves to the Ibans with divine reasons. Sandin (1980, p.xxxiii) mentions that, the appearance and behaviour of the birds are interpreted according to symbolic representations comprising a system of signs based on which specific meaning is construed into the birds' calls, flight or other forms of manners. Sandin (1980, p.xxxv) further adds,

"[a]s a general rule, the meaning assigned to a particular call depends not only on the bird that utters it, but also on the context in which it is heard; the direction from which the sound comes, whether from the left, right, front or back of the hearer, and whether it is heard alone or in a sequence, preceded or followed within a short time by the calls of other augural birds."

Therefore, it is the duty of the Iban individuals to pay cautious attention to these signs by interpreting their meaning accurately that serve as their guide to their own conducts following their designations. Hence, the tendency to observe and interpret the natural world indicates a strong concrete relationship between the Iban self and nature.

Conclusion

In sum, this chapter offers the insights to the concept of emotions across cultures, a well as the background information on the world of the Ibans. The understanding of the Ibans' world, particularly their language and culture, is essential in the discussion of this research study. Apparently, the Ibans' world is centralized around the communal living of the longhouse, of where they devote their personal and social lives to the people around them. Devotions are not only paid to the society alone, but also to the natural surroundings as well. Notably, the Ibans' devotions are deeply confined by the rules of *adat*—a system which governs the personal and social conducts of every Iban person. Drawing from the information, we could further define the Ibans' interactional and communicative style with others, and venture into their world of perception, which no doubt is unique and exhaustive.

Figure 2: An Iban girl dressed in all the finery of the traditional costume

Figure 3: An Iban man clad in a traditional costume[6]

---

[6]   The picture is taken from my personal collection, which illustrates my late grandfather.

Figure 4: Iban headmen in their ritual costumes during a *gawai* feast

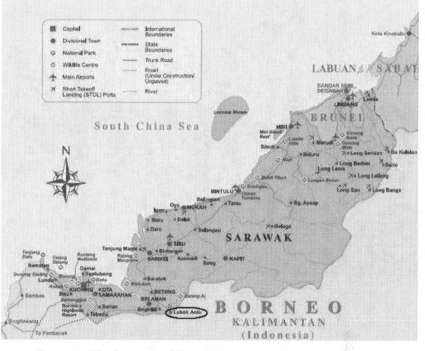

Figure 5: The location of Sbangki Panjai on the map of Sarawak
(source: www.curtin.edu.my)

Figure 6: The longhouse of Sbangki Panjai in Lubok Antu, Sarawak[7]

---

[7] The image of the longhouse does not resemble the structure of the traditional one—a traditional longhouse is constructed on stilts using timber and leaf thatches as the roof. Sbangki Panjai Longhouse is primarily built using modern materials, such as bricks and cement, which give it a strong, concrete and contemporary look. The picture above illustrates the front of the longhouse exterior part, showing a long stretched cemented veranda or walkway, called the *tanju*.

Figure 7: The *tanju* (veranda or walkway)
This structure serves as a place for putting the paddy
or black pepper to dry before being stored.

Figure 8: The living room in an Iban *bilik*[8]

Figure 9: The dining room in an Iban *bilik*

---

[8]   The picture above displays a contemporary concept which does not reflect the traditional longhouse living.

Figure 10: An opening in the kitchen—this structure is commonly found in a longhouse kitchen which provides inter-communication between the family *biliks* of the longhouse

Figure 11: The *ruai* (corridor)

Figure 12: The *ruai* also functions as a communal
hall for traditional religious rituals.

Figure 13: The *ruai* also serves as a meeting place for the head
men to discuss issues pertaining to longhouse daily matters.

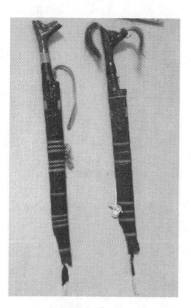

(a) *Ilang*   (b) *Bebendai* (upper) and *tawak* (lower)

(c) *Tajau* (jars)

Figure 14: Some valuable items in an Iban *bilik*

(a) *Ilang*—this is a special knife which was used as a war weapon during the headhunting days; however, after the headhunting practice was made illegal, it now serves as a cutting knife for daily purposes, such as for chopping meat and woods, or simply displayed on the wall for decorative purpose.

(b) *Bebendai* (upper) and *tawak* (lower)—both items are among valuable brassware in an Iban *bilik* that serve many functions, namely, as wedding gifts in the traditional Iban culture and as musical percussion instruments hit with a mallet during *gawai* festivals.

(c) *Tajau* (jars)—the *tajau* serves many functions, for instance, as a storage for rice and water; in the ancient Iban traditions, it was also used as a dowry in the community's marriage customs.

Figure 15: The *pelabuh* (the hut)

The structure above used to house the enemies' heads or *antu pala*; however, after a majority of the Ibans at Sbangki Panjai converted to Christianity, the human heads were taken to the jungle and given proper burial rites by the village folks.

Figure 16: An Iban woman attending to her newly grown black
pepper orchard; black pepper is one of the cash crops planted
by the Ibans apart from rubber tree and oil palm.

Figure 17: The hill paddy is a major crop cultivated
by the Ibans at Sbangki Panjai.

CHAPTER III

RESEARCH METHODOLOGY

Research Design

This research was carried out through interviews, my own personal observation and library research. The Iban speakers were interviewed on the topic of emotion concepts in Iban culture. With reference to 'borrowing' of words, the respondents were also asked why they opted to borrow words from other languages, and their attitudes towards their language.

Subjects

The respondents of this study were the Iban native speakers from the longhouse of Sbangki Panjai, Lubok Antu, Sarawak, which is located in the rural area of Sri Aman division, approximately 67 kilometres from the town of Sri Aman (see Figure 5). Needless to say, I am also an origin of the longhouse; therefore, there were no issues pertaining to the access to the Iban community at the longhouse while carrying out this research study. The Iban folks, aged between 20 to 80 years old, were casually interviewed with regard to how they express their emotions to others. I also carried out my own personal observation on how the emotion concepts were expressed in the respondents' daily conduct.

The Ibans in Sbangki Panjai mostly work as hill-rice farmers, as well as black pepper and rubber tree planters. These people are exceptionally busy farmers; they work in the field as early as five o'clock in the morning and return home at 6 o'clock in the evening. After dinner approximately at 7 o'clock, the villagers normally sit at the *ruai* to relax, plat mat or basket, weave *pua kumbu*, or simply chat and gossip before retrieving to their *biliks* at 8 o'clock in the evening. Normally by 9, all the lights in the longhouse will be switched off.

Procedure

As mentioned earlier, the native speakers were casually interviewed and asked questions as to how they express their emotions in the Iban language. During the casual interview sessions, the respondents were provided examples of expressions in the Iban language. The interviews were exclusively conducted in Iban since I am also a speaker of the language. The elicitation of data was done by giving the Iban speakers situations and asking them to react as if they were in them. In addition, they were also asked about their attitudes towards the Malay language and English. Apart from the casual interviews, I also carried out my personal observations on the social interactions among the dwellers of the longhouse.

Analysis of Data

The explications, analyses and interpretations of the Iban emotion concepts in this study were discussed within the framework of the concrete/abstract cultural continuum, as well as the Natural Semantic Metalanguage, as the instrument for linguistic analysis. The following section will further elaborate the framework and instrument used in this research work.

Cultural Continuum

D'Cruz and Steele (2000) and earlier D'Cruz and Tham (1993) have developed a framework around the notions of concrete/abstract cultural continuum. They state that "cultures can be usefully related and described by means of notionally locating them on a continuum of which the twin poles are the metaphors of 'concreteness' and 'abstraction'" (D'Cruz & Steele, 2000, p.92). The following figure illustrates the cultural continuum:

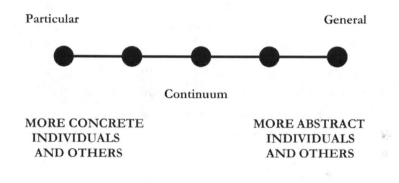

Figure 18: Cultural Continuum

The location of one's culture in the continuum largely determines the type of person that individual belongs to. However, as D'Cruz and Steele (2000) state, there are no pure types of culture; at all times, there are only more concrete or more abstract societies along a cultural continuum. The following sections further define the concepts of concrete and abstract cultures.

Concrete Culture

D'Cruz and Steele (2000) point out that the more concrete cultures are located towards the more concrete end of the continuum. These cultures are oriented towards a set of values which tend to co-exist. This set of values includes, "the privileging of the group over the individual (and with it a consensually hierarchical rather than egalitarian social form and ethic), the claims of kinship or blood relationship over an all-encompassing but attenuated love, respect for wisdom that arises out of experience rather than expert knowledge issuing from an objectivised stance, group loyalty and claims of group privacy over individual privacy, partnership with rather than subjugation of the natural world, problem resolution methods favouring face-to-face contact yet often relying on an indirect style requiring interpretation of the unsaid, and a preference for the near and tangible in all areas (thus, the redistribution of income through gift-giving rather than taxation, commerce by barter rather than money, social intercourse with neighbours according to local custom rather than with a geographically far-flung network of contacts operating on a shared ethical and/or interest base, perhaps using social extended forms of contact as with (say) strangers through the Internet, etc.)."

(D'Cruz & Steele, 2000, p.92)

In other words, members of the more concrete cultures share a strong sense of belonging in their community. Kim, Sharkey and Singelis (1994) point out that this more concrete notion can be associated with the term 'collectivism'. Collectivism emphasizes the importance of the collective—that is,

"the tendency to be more concerned about the consequences of one's behaviour for in-group members and to be more willing to sacrifice personal interests for the attainment of collective interests and harmony."

(Kim, Sharkey & Singelis, 1994, p.122)

In addition, Hofstede (1994) states that collectivism pertains to communities in which the societal members are integrated into strong, cohesive in-groups from their birth onwards, and this integration continues to protect them in exchange for unquestioning loyalty throughout their lifetime. Their loyalty is geared towards the group and interdependent with one another. Furthermore, their interdependence also signifies the relationship of self with others, which is an attribute of concrete cultures, such as in the Iban community. Members of this culture are the significant products of the concrete relationships in which they are engaged in. They know and recognize one another as members of the group, family or clan. Their identities, thus, depend on which community or society they belong to. The identity of more concrete individuals is defined more in terms of kindred relationships, for instance, "I am the mother of X", "I am a member of family Y", and "I am a resident of Z" (Triandis, 1989, p.514).

Individuals with more concrete attributes are directed towards maintaining a group's harmony in their relationship with others (Condon & Yousef, 1975; Kim, Sharkey, Singelis, 1994). They have the tendency to sacrifice their individual interests in order to maintain group or kinship harmony, as well as solidarity. They tend to view issues in relational terms, bearing in mind that every action, judgement, evaluation, observation and measurement that they make is significantly related to themselves and the 'particular' others, or between the people concerned, particularly family members, clans, ethnic groups, and so forth. In addition, members of the more concrete culture come together in a community or society, whereby the concern is to maintain hierarchy within their memberships (Wierzbicka, 1991).

Abstract Culture

In contrast to the concrete culture, the abstract culture is located towards the abstract end of the cultural continuum. D'Cruz and Steele (2000, p.93) state that,

"the more abstract culture (or individual) will emphasise and value individuality, and privilege the individual's free choice in democratic practices even if as individuals it means to stand against the state and one's own community. Also valued are autonomy, disengaged rationality, all-encompassing love, professionalism, direct communication styles yet mediated relationships (often without face-to-face contact), money (often in particularly intangible forms, such as equities) and so on."

A more abstract individual views independence, autonomy, freedom, and privacy as amongst his or her most important values. Members of this culture relate themselves to the generalized others, and they come together as volunteered individuals in networks, for example, as civil workers or government servants. Unlike the more concrete people, the individuals claim to be in charge of their own selves. Only they alone have the right to control their own beings, which means, they have the tendency to view themselves as the only 'real' persons, while others are those who exist on their own. They become their own judge to their actions, measure their own potential, and self-govern their own choices or preferences. For instance, the Anglo-American principle of turn-taking can be seen as a manifestation of the more abstract concept of equality, or the principle of personal autonomy and respect for an individual's rights.

Moreover, individuals with abstract attributes are also inclined to express their desires, dislikes and thoughts without restraint. Furthermore, in the Anglo-American culture, there is less (if any) emphasis on 'we', instead, the weight is more on every individual's disconnected and autonomous 'I'. This justifies the claim that the more abstract individuals only view themselves as the 'real' beings, while other people are perceived as 'generalized' objects (Wierzbicka, 1991). Besides, a more abstract person tends to emphasize elements of identity that reflect possessions and professionalism, such as 'What do I own', 'What experience do I had', and 'What are my accomplishments' (Triandis, 1989; D'Cruz & Steele, 2000). Hence, their goals are normally directed towards personal self-actualization or self-development. Their loyalty, thus, is projected towards this autonomous identity. We can further associate this abstract notion to what Triandis (1989, p.512) terms as "the tendency to be more concerned about one's behaviour for one's own needs, interests, and goals."

A person who grows up in an individualistic culture will have the tendency to emphasize self-reliance, autonomy and self-actualization. Therefore, members of this individualistic or abstract culture can be assumed as strongly in charge of their own selves, such as when it comes to decision making (Condon & Yousef, 1975; Kim, Sharkey, & Singelis, 1994).

Natural Semantic Metalanguage (NSM)

Natural Semantic Metalanguage (NSM) is an analytical tool established on the principles of clarity and simplicity. It was introduced by the Polish scholar, Andrzej Boguslawski, in Eastern Europe in the 1960s. Subsequently, Anna Wierzbicka developed and extended the theory with detailed elaborations. Wierzbicka (1980) describes NSM as the notion that we possess a mental language ("lingua mentalis") beyond our specific verbal languages ("linguae vocals, linguae gentium").

NSM consists of a small set of simple meanings, whereby evidence suggests that they can be articulated using words or bound morphemes in all languages, for example, PEOPLE, SOMEONE, SOMETHING, THIS, SAY, THINK, WANT, KNOW, GOOD, BAD, NO and so forth. These words emerge to be lexical universals with meanings that can be translated accurately between all languages in the world. When joint with a small set of universal grammatical patterns, these words or bound morphemes become an ideal analytical tool for examining cross-linguistic semantics (Goddard, 1997; Wierzbicka, 1980). Goddard (1997, p.185) further stresses that,

"the metalanguage of lexical universals can be used not only for semantic analysis, but also to formulate cultural 'rules' which Wierzbicka proposes to call 'cultural scripts'. Because they are phrased in simple and translatable terms, such scripts can achieve a high degree of precision while at the same time minimizing the danger of ethnocentric bias creeping into the very terms of the description."

An ideal NSM semantic analysis (often called an 'explication') is a paraphrase expressed in the simplest possible terminologies which aims to prevent circular and obscure translations or interpretations. The explication in NSM does not comprise technical terms, extravagant terminologies, logic representations or short forms. Instead, it only includes simple expressions from the ordinary natural language. Because it is supposed to represent a thorough paraphrase, the semantic analysis is exhaustive and comprehensive so as to reveal the complete meaning of the expression being examined without creating ethnocentric bias. NSM is also based on the expectation that an explication expressed in simple semantic words can be readily decoded across human languages (Wierzbicka, 1992; Goddard, 1998).

Following the necessity to decrease ethnocentric bias in explaining cultural means of interacting, NSM is suggested in order to improve the descriptive accuracy of cultural translations and interpretations, as well as to facilitate the integration of pragmatics and cultural semantics in the linguistic analysis. NSM also assists in discovering and exposing the relations between specific ways of interacting and cultural values, as well as the people's attitudes concerned. According to Goddard (1997), this theory of 'cultural scripts' provides substantial answers to the problems of explaining speech patterns meticulously and accurately, recognising the pertinent cultural values and attributes independently of the speech patterns themselves, and most of all, reducing ethnocentric judgment that will possibly alter the pragmatic meaning of the terminologies being explained.

The conventional metalanguage utilised for describing cultural communicative norms comprises a set of open-ended technical and semi-technical terms, for instance, 'directness', 'formality', 'politeness', 'involvement', 'face', and so forth. Although these terms are useful to a certain degree, they are not free from critiques for being somewhat fuzzy. Different scholars or authors often employ these terms with different meanings. For example, there is a variation with regard to the concept of indirectness and directness in Japanese and English cultures. In comparing these two cultures, the Japanese are viewed as 'indirect' while the English as 'direct'. However, when it comes to the comparison between English and Hebrew, it is the English that are perceived as 'indirect' instead, whereas the Hebrew as 'direct'. Thus, cultures of the world vary in looking at the notion of indirectness and directness. These differences in cultural perception consist of the areas or encounters that require indirectness, the guidelines or rules of how to be indirect, and the reason(s) for being indirect when interacting with others (Goddard, 1997). Therefore, NSM is believed to be the answer to the problem of explaining the cultural ways of interacting.

NSM is an essential method that enables us to carry out linguistic analyses on words cross-culturally, and it also facilitates in avoiding Anglo-centric bias in describing culture-specific terminologies. For instance, the English words 'thank' and 'apology' do not integrate well in the Japanese culture. One may marvel what the Japanese people would do in occasions which require them to apologize when expressing their regret, or thank someone when showing their gratitude. In a general sense, the verb 'to thank' means to utter one's good feeling towards the other person for the good thing that the person has accomplished for him or her. With reference to the European cultures, uttering the word 'thanks' or 'thank you' is a standard response when a favour or gift is received. However, this European norm seems to deviate in the Japanese culture, which stresses social hierarchy and obligatory repayment (reciprocity) of all favours. In other words, it is a tradition for the Japanese people to react to the favour they receive similar to the way they respond when they have transgressed someone (Wierzbicka, 1992). Thus, rather than uttering one's 'good feeling' for the favour or gift received (for instance), one would express his or her 'bad feeling' instead. The expression such as *sumimasen*, which literally means 'it never ends' (i.e. 'I am aware of my 'never-ending indebtedness' to you'), is used both in communicative encounters which closely match with the English words 'thank' and 'apology' for expressing gratification and regrets. In fact, the Japanese language does not have a verb equivalent to the English verb 'thank'. The nearest word it has is *kansha kuru,* which originates from the Chinese language. However, the Japanese will not use the word in specific situations, for instance, when a child thanks her mother for a present, or when a lecturer thanks her student for some task. The use of the word is virtually constrained to written language only. The non-existence of the speech act 'thank' in Japanese signifies the importance of status, position and the form of relationship in terms of the way one responds to an act of kindness (Wierzbicka, 1992).

As mentioned earlier, NSM allows a cross-culture comparison of words in human languages. Hence, by translating both the English word 'thank' and the Japanese word *kansha kuru* into the metalanguage of universal semantic primitives, we can reveal the similarities and discrepancies of the words. The following explications illustrate both words:

thank
I know: you did something good for me
I feel something good towards you because of this
I say this because I want you to feel something good

kansha kuru
I know: you did something good for me
I say: I feel something good towards you because of this
I know: I couldn't do something good like this for you
I feel something bad because of this
I say this because I think I should say it

(Wierzbicka, 1992)

NSM makes it possible to sketch the links between indigenous cultural values and rules of speaking, such as those found in Iban. For example[9], the emotion terminology of *malu* carries many social meanings in the Iban culture. The term is often glossed as 'ashamed', 'shy' or 'embarrassed' in English. However, drawing from the meaning and context of Iban culture, *malu* is a feeling which is closely similar to the feelings of 'shame', 'modesty' and 'propriety'. The following explication further illustrates the emotion concept:

---

[9]   The example is drawn from the research data of this study. The analysis of the emotion expression of *malu* is further explained in Chapter 4.

X feels *malu* =
X thinks something like this:
    people can know something about me
    people can think something bad about me because of this
    people can say something bad about me because of this
    I don't want this
because of this, X wants not to be near people
because of all this, X feels something bad

In addition, another social meaning of *malu* is that, it indicates one's negative reaction to the idea that other people could think something (anything) bad about one. Thus, *malu* is associated with the feelings of 'modesty' and 'humility'; it denotes a person's good feelings upon being teased or being given compliments, for instance.

The explication below illustrates the emotion concept:

X feels *malu* =
X thinks something like this (about Y):
    I know Y did something good for me
    it is good for Y to do something like this
    I feel something good towards Y because of this
    I want Y to know this, not because I say anything about it
    If Y can see me, Y will know how I feel
because of this, X feels something good

Based on this theory, the Iban emotion terminologies will be explicated using NSM in order to achieve thorough and precise speech pattern descriptions, identify relevant cultural values and priorities independently of the Iban speech patterns, and minimize ethnocentric bias.

CHAPTER IV

SOCIAL EMOTIONS AND EXPRESSIONS IN IBAN

Introduction

The Iban speakers from Sbangki Panjai Longhouse, Lubok Antu, Sarawak, were interviewed in the course of this research. It was revealed that all the respondents produced similar types of answers to the situations[10] given. Needless to say, these similar speech patterns indicate that the speakers were from the same speech community. However, it must be noted that in terms of borrowing, there was a strong tendency among the younger respondents to use loanwords from Malay and English, such as *ampun*, *terima kasih*, 'sorry', and 'thank you', respectively, when it comes to the emotional expressions of the kinds.

Several emotion concepts in Iban culture as obtained from the respondents will be highlighted in this chapter. The results were tabled and grouped to ease data inspection, as follows.

---

[10]   The interview questions are outlined in APPENDIX A.

Table 2: Expressions of anger, shame, disgust and surprise

Situation	Emotional Expression			
	anger	shame	disgust	surprise
How do you feel if someone hurts your feeling and does not bother to apologize?	*pedis ati* *ringat* *ransi* *kudi*		*begedi* *benchi* *bebulu ati*	
How do you feel when you find out that someone you really trust betrays you?	*pedis ati* *ringat* *ransi* *kudi*		*begedi* *benchi* *bebulu ati*	*tekenyit* *abis ati*
Someone humiliates you in front of others (e.g. say nasty things about you), how do you describe your feeling at that moment?	*pedis ati* *ringat* *ransi* *kudi*	*malu*	*begedi* *benchi* *bebulu ati*	*tekenyit* *abis ati*

Table 3: Expression of gratitude/joy

Situation	Emotion of Gratitude/Joy
How do you feel after someone has just granted you a favour?	(i) No words are needed. It is assumed that the other person understands the concept of 'thank you' in Iban; giving a smile is more than enough. (ii) Sometimes, the other party will return the favour or gift as a means of expressing his or her gratitude.
Someone has given you something (e.g. food, a souvenir, money), what is/are the word/words that you use to describe your gratitude towards her/him?	No words are needed. It is assumed that the other person understands the concept of 'thank you' in Iban; giving a smile is more than enough.
You have just won a competition. How do you describe your feeling at the moment?	*gaga* *andal*

Table 4: Expression of love/affection

Situation	Emotion of Love/Affection
How do you describe your affection to someone you love?	*sayau* *rindu*
You really fancy someone. How do you describe your feeling for her/him?	*sayau* *rindu*
How do you say 'I love you' in Iban to a specific person you really love?	*Aku sayau ka di'.*

Table 5: Expression of loneliness

Situation	Expression of Loneliness
You have not seen your love one for a long time and you terribly miss her/him. How do you describe your feeling at that moment?	*lelengau* *seilu-ilu*

Table 6: Expression of guilt

Situation	Expression of Guilt
You realize you have hurt someone's feeling. How do you make up with her/him?	Just keep quiet and hope that the person will forgive her/him; or he/she could do him/her a favour in order to make up for the mistake.
How do you say 'I'm sorry' in Iban?	sorry *minta ampun*

Table 7: Expression of fear

Situation	Expression of Fear
What do you call a person's attitude when he or she is afraid or scared of darkness?	*buyan*

Table 8: Expression of sympathy

Situation	Emotion Expression	
	sympathy	surprise
Your close friend has received a bad news. How do you feel towards her or him?	*sinu* *kasih*	
You come across an old beggar with an amputated leg. How do you feel towards him?	*sinu* *kasih*	
You have received a bad news that someone close to you has passed away. How do you describe your feeling at that moment?		*tekenyit* *abis ati*

For the sake of convenience, the following table groups the emotion terminologies in Iban as obtained from the respondents.

Table 9: The Iban emotion terminologies

Emotion Expressions	Iban Emotion Terminologies
anger	*pedis ati, ringat, ransi, kudi*
shame	*malu*
disgust	*begedi, benchi, bebulu ati*
surprise	*abis ati, tekenyit*
gratitude/joy	*gaga, andal*
love/affection	*sayau, rindu*
loneliness	*lelengau, seilu-ilu*
guilt	sorry, *minta ampun*
fear	*buyan*
sympathy	*sinu, kasih*

The table below indicates the loanwords in Iban emotion terminologies (Richards, 1981; Sutlive, 1994; Wilkinson, 1958; Winstedt, 1967):

Table 10: Loanwords in Iban

Language	Loanwords in Iban
	terima kasih
	minta ampun
	kasih
Malay	*ringat*
	benchi
	sayau
	pedis ati
English	thank you
	sorry

Many terms are used to describe anger in Iban, such as *pedis ati, ringat, ransi, kudi,* and *angat.* In addition, there is also a certain degree of anger in Iban according to how angry the person is at any moment. While the terms *pedis ati, ringat* and *ransi* indicate mild versions of anger, the expression of *kudi* denotes a strong version of the feeling that is more intense. *Kudi* also means 'a storm' in Iban. Hence, as characterised by the presence of lightning and thunder during a storm, the emotion expression of *kudi* is equivalent to the turbulent weather, giving the impression that the person is in extreme anger. When one is *kudi,* he tends to throw tantrums, even to the extent of running amok. In the past, a *kudi* person would even declare a war by performing headhunting on the other party as a way of seeking revenge. Therefore, it can be assumed that in the traditional Iban culture, 'anger' is the driving force behind the warring attribute of the Iban people.

With regard to the term *malu,* other than being associated with the feeling of 'shame' or 'embarrassment', *malu* also denotes the attributes of 'modesty', 'propriety' and 'shyness' in Iban.

On the other hand, words of 'thanks' are hardly expressed in Iban culture. When one is gratified upon being given something or granted a favour, verbal expressions are normally unuttered to the other party. Instead, facial expressions, such as smiling, are used in response. Sometimes, an Iban individual may return or exchange the favour or gift as a means of conveying his or her gratitude. Furthermore, in order to say 'thanks' in Iban, the person may express his or her gratitude by complimenting the other party for being fortunate to have such a gift. The following utterances exemplify several expressions of the emotion:

1. *Untung amai di'!*
   (What a lucky person you are!)
2. *Dini di' bulih tu?*
   (Where did you get this?)
3. *Manah amai utai tu!*
   (What a lovely thing!)

Likewise, when one wishes to express his or her affection/love to someone, words of intimacy are normally not verbalized. Instead, body gestures, such as eye contact and presentation of a gift, are used. This norm conforms to the Ibans' restriction in displaying their emotional expressions explicitly.

In the Iban culture, there are no words for 'apology'. In fact, apologies are non-existent and not accepted in this culture. Instead, the guilty person has to pay his or her fine to the other party, which is associated with the Iban custom of *adat*. It is the *adat* that determines the fate of a person.

Similar to the expression of anger in Iban, the expressions of love/affection, loneliness, and sympathy also have a certain degree in them. For instance, the terms *rindu* and *sayau* are variably expressed in accordance with the degree of affection in the person. *Rindu*, on the other hand, is used for anybody whether or not that person is fond of him or her, whereas *sayau* specifically refers to someone that the person is really intimate with. Meanwhile, *seilu-ilu* carries a deeper meaning of loneliness as compared to *lelengau*. Similarly, *sinu* also brings a deeper meaning of sympathy as compared to the term *kasih*.

Expressions such as *sorry* and *minta ampun* are not of Iban origin (see Table 11 and Table 12 for other examples of loanwords); they are borrowed from English and Malay, respectively. In expressing these emotion words, the Ibans normally resort to non-verbal communication or utterances of indirect speech.

Interpretations and Explications of the Ibans' Social Emotions and Expressions

One of the aims of this research work is to explicate the Iban emotion concepts using NSM. The Iban emotion concepts can be traced back to the Malay culture due to the fact that both cultures come from the same stock of Proto Malays. In fact, both cultures seem to resemble one another in many aspects of their lifestyles. The following sections will describe and explicate several terms of the emotion concepts.

The Social Emotion of *Malu*

The social emotion of *malu* in Iban is closely translated as 'shame', 'modesty' and 'propriety' (as already mentioned in Chapter 3). However, in bilingual dictionaries, *malu* is often referred to as 'ashamed', 'shy', or 'embarrassed'. Nevertheless, *malu* carries many social meanings in Iban culture.

Firstly, the emotion of *malu* is a negative reaction to the idea that other people could think something (anything) bad about one. Moreover, *malu* is a prospect that is of great unpleasantness to any Iban's sensibility. Some examples of the expression of *malu* as given by the respondents are as follows:

1. ***Malu*** *amai aku meda perangai di'.*
   (I am ashamed to see your behaviour.)
2. *Anang meri **malu** ngagai bilik kitai!*
   (Don't you bring shame to our family!)

To describe the emotion of *malu* in Iban, the following explication is presented:

X feels *malu* =
X thinks something like this:
    people can know something about me
    people can think something bad about me because of this
    people can say something bad about me because of this
    I don't want this
because of this, X wants not to be near people
because of all this, X feels something bad

Secondly, although the expression of *malu* is also glossed as 'embarrassed' in English, it does not only indicate bad feelings in the person. Unlike the English term 'embarrassed' which denotes the negative feeling of humiliation, the term *malu* in Iban is closely akin to the feelings of modesty and humility. In addition, the expression of *malu* indicates a person's good feelings upon being teased or given compliments. When one is *malu*, one will normally blush and look downward in order to conceal one's emotion. This is normally the case when young girls are being teased by young boys during courtship. *Malu* is also the result when compliments are received. Instead of thanking the other person for the compliment, the normal reaction is to shy down and deflect the remark. The following present some examples of this emotion expression as obtained from the respondents:

1. *Ia agi **malu** ka di'.*
   (She is still shy of you.)
2. *Endu enggai pansut ari bilik laban **malu** ka di'.*
   (Endu does not want to come out from the room because she is shy of you.)
3. *Nyau **malu** sida indu dara ditundi bala sida bujang.*
   (The lasses were shy upon being teased by the lads.)

The explication below illustrates the other concept of *malu*:

X feels *malu* =
X thinks something like this (about Y):
    I know Y did something good for me
    it is good for Y to do something like this
    I feel something good towards Y because of this
    I want Y to know this, not because I say anything about it
    If Y can see me, Y will know how I feel
because of this, X feels something good

The Social Emotions of *Pedis Ati, Ransi, Ringat* and *Kudi*

It is interesting to note that the social emotion of 'anger' in Iban appears in many forms. Similar to the Malay emotion of *marah,* the Iban emotions of *pedis ati* and *ransi* can also be referred to the term as well.

Western viewers are mostly puzzled with both terms, in which they are often translated as 'angry' in bilingual dictionaries. Although the English 'angry' and the Iban *pedis ati* and *ransi* are unlikeable reactions to the perception that someone has done something wrong, the prototypical description of the abovementioned Iban emotion terms is so different that English words such as 'offended' and 'resentful' are seemingly more precise in describing their semantic explanation as compared to the term 'angry'. The terms are associated with the Ibans' tendency to be easily offended or upset but reluctant to express their feelings openly. Thus, instead of bursting hostile words and displaying physical reactions characteristic of 'anger', the people tend to linger in sullen brooding, which is an expression of emotion described as *ringat*. Similar to the Malay term *merajuk,* when one is *ringat,* he or she tends to stay sullen for a period of time which can last for hours, days, weeks, months or even years before his or her *ringat* recedes (Goddard, 1998).

At first, the concepts of *pedis ati* and *ransi* appear to be equivalent with the English word 'angry', which refer to the thought that one has done something bad to another person. But a closer investigation shows that there is something more personal about the terms, which is more akin to the English word 'offended' than the word 'angry'. People are often described as *pedis ati* or *ransi* as a consequence of being disrespectfully treated or humiliated. As stated by Goddard (1998), taking it personally indicates a significant feature of the prototypical states of *pedis ati* and *ransi*. In addition, the emotion concepts are closely associated with disgusted feelings, thus resulting in the concept of face saving or *jaga mua* in Iban. The following utterances describe the emotional feelings of *pedis ati* and *ransi*:

1. *Ia **ransi** ka aku ketegal aku enggai meri ia duit.*
   (He is mad at me because I refuse to give him money.)
2. ***Pedis ati** aku ngenang jako di'.*
   (I am angry when I recall the words you said.)

The emotion concepts of *pedis ati* and *ransi* can be further illustrated in the following explication:

X is *pedis ati/ransi* (to Y) =
Sometimes a person thinks something like this (about Y):
>   Y did something bad
>   Y knows I do not want Y to do something like this
>   I feel something bad because of that
>   I want Y to know this, not because I say anything about it
because of this, X feels something bad

Consequently, the concept of face saving or *jaga mua* in Iban can also be compared to the English concepts of 'dignity', 'self-respect', 'pride' and the like. This range of translation proposes that *jaga mua* involves what others think about one and what one thinks about oneself. *Jaga mua* is also equivalent to the concept of *jaga adat* in Iban culture, in which both concepts reveal an implication of the moral, that is, *jaga mua* and *jaga adat* suggest one's intentional declination to commit wrongdoings. In other words, both concepts posit that one has to be mindful of his or her behavioural conducts in the public domain. The following explication further illustrates the meaning of *jaga mua*:

jaga mua
X thinks something like this:
>   I know people can't think about me:
>>   'this person is not a good person'
>>   'this person does bad things'
>   it is good for a person if a person can think some things like this

Another expression of 'anger' in Iban is *kudi*. In contrast to the terms *pedis ati* and *ringat*, *kudi* is used to express a strong degree of 'anger'. As mentioned earlier, the term *kudi* also means 'a storm' in the Iban language. Hence, the expression of *kudi* is likened to the bad weather, in which a *kudi* person may display tantrums and sometimes an outburst of hostile words. When one is *kudi,* his or her state of 'anger' is parallel to that of the expression as presented below:

Ia **kudi** *amai sampai abis barang rumah nya diperunsai ka ia.*
(He is so angry that all the things in the house were turned upside down by him.)

The following explication is also given to illustrate the term:

X feels *kudi* =
X thinks something like this:
    I know Y did something to me
    it is bad for Y to do something like this
    I feel something bad towards Y because of this
    I want Y to know this, not because I say anything about it
    if Y can see me, Y will know how I feel
because of this, X feels something bad

In the traditional Iban culture, a *kudi* person often resulted in him seeking revenge by declaring *kayau* (headhunting) on the transgressor. The state of 'anger' in an Iban person was believed to be the driving force behind the warring spirit of the ancient traditional Iban culture. Furthermore, when one is a victim of the transgressor, the transgressor has to pay a fine or reparation in order to make up for his or her wrong act(s). More often, words of apology will not be accepted to make up for the offence that a transgressor has committed. Therefore, to settle any misunderstanding or dispute between members of the Iban community, *adat* will ultimately speak for both. As mentioned earlier in Chapter 2, *adat* refers broadly to rules, canons and sanctions that function to ensure a continuation of harmonious relationship among the Iban community members. This concept of *adat* can be explicated as follows:

adat

X thinks something like this:

before I say/do something to someone, it is good to think:

I don't want this person to feel something bad because of this

I don't want this person to think something bad about me

I don't want this person to say something bad about me

because of this, I don't want this

I have to think about what I say/do before I say/do it

because of this, X doesn't say/do some things

When a person has been offended by someone else, it is expected of him or her to ask for *adat* (*minta adat*), which means, he or she has the right to request for a compensation in accordance with what the *adat* has stipulated. To ensure fair execution of justice, it is the responsibility of the *tuai rumah* (the longhouse headman) and other senior members of the Iban community to see that accurate fines and ritual conducts are applied and every redress act is made. This is to ensure that *adat* is maintained which will eventually result in the restoration of social harmony and spiritual health of the whole Iban community.

The Emotion Expressions of *Benchi, Begedi* and *Bebulu Ati*

The terms *benchi, begedi* and *bebulu ati* are emotion expressions which are closely related to the expression of 'anger' in the Iban culture. While *benchi* denotes the mild version of 'hatred', *begedi* and *bebulu ati* bear the strong version of the emotion. When one has this emotional feeling (i.e. *benchi*) for someone, one will convey his or her bad feeling to the other person, even to the extent of refusing to see the person's sight. This bad feeling is never uttered verbally but reserved by the person. However, expressions of *benchi, begedi* and *bebulu ati* could be traced by seeing the person's non-verbal reactions, such as displayed through his or her facial expressions. Normally, a person's wrong acts cause these feelings to occur. The examples below are presented as given by the respondents:

1. *Aku **benchi** meda perangai di' ti enda menuku.*
   (I hate to see your bad behaviour.)
2. *Naka meh **begedi** ati ia meda anembiak nya ketegal enda bebasa ka orang tuai.*
   (He is so angry to see the child's behaviour of not respecting the elderly.)
3. *Udah ia ti ngaga penyalah nya, **bebulu ati** aku meda ia.*
   (After he has committed the offence, I despise the sight of him.)

The terms *benchi, begedi* and *bebulu ati* can be explicated as follows:

X feels *benchi/begedi/bebulu ati* =
sometimes a person thinks something like this (about Y):
    Y did something bad
    Y knows I do not want Y to do something like this
    I feel something bad because of that
    I feel something bad towards Y because of that
    I want Y to know this, not because I say anything about it
    if Y can see me, Y will know how I feel
because of this, X feels something bad
X feels like this

The Social Expression of Gratitude

There are no words for 'thank you' in the Iban culture. In contrast to the English culture which encourages the people to verbally express their gratitude upon receiving gifts, favours, or compliments, the Iban culture discourages the verbal expression of this emotion. On accepting a gift or favour, it would be unlikely for one to say anything like 'thank you'. Instead, to acknowledge the other person's act of kindness, expressions of compliment are ascribed to the presentation of the gift as exemplified by the utterances below:

1. *Untung amai di'!*
   (You are so lucky!)
2. *Dini di' bulih tu?*
   (Where did you get this?)
3. *Manah amai utai tu!*
   (What a lovely thing!)

The expression of gratitude is often transmitted through non-verbal behaviours or facial expressions (e.g. returning the favour, exchanging the gift, smiling, etc.). This non-verbal communication explains that in Iban concrete or high context culture, it is understood that the receiving party is gratified with the gift, favour or compliment even though there is no utterance of verbal words. The Iban people are very adept at reading non-verbal behaviours. The expressions can be explicated into two parts as follows:

(i) on receiving a gift or favour:
　　　　X thinks something like this (about Y):
　　　　　　I know Y did something good for me
　　　　　　it is good for Y to do something like this
　　　　　　I feel something good towards Y because of this
　　　　　　I want Y to know this, not because I say anything about it
　　　　X feels like this

(ii) non-verbal expression (e.g. smile) on receiving a compliment:
　　　　X thinks something like this (about Y):
　　　　　　when I feel something
　　　　　　I don't want to say how I feel to Y
　　　　　　it is not good to say 'I feel like this'
　　　　　　if Y can see me, Y will know how I feel
　　　　X feels like this

Because there are no words of 'thank you' in the Iban language, most Iban people nowadays tend to borrow from other languages, such as

Malay and English. The phenomenon of borrowing, in fact, has become an important means of expressing emotions in Iban. Instead of merely giving the other person a non-verbal expression (e.g. a smile), words of *terima kasih* or 'thank you' are used as a way of acknowledging the person's act of kindness. The explication below further illustrates this emotion of gratitude:

> *terima kasih*/thank you
> X thinks something like this:
>> I know you did something good for me
>> it is good for you to do something like this
>> I feel something good towards you because of this
>> I say this because I should say it
> because of this, X feels something good

Another means of expressing gratitude whenever a compliment is received is by deflecting the remarks. For example, when one compliments a person on her dress, the normal response is to deflect the remark by saying the following:

> *Gari' utai lama tu'.*
> (This is an old dress.)

According to Wierzbicka (1991), different cultures give different responses to compliments. Wierzbicka argues that the deflection of remarks is not a characteristic of one's 'lack of confidence' as claimed by the Western view. Instead of saying the words 'thank you' which Westerners think is an appropriate and standard response whenever a compliment is given, some cultures deflect the remarks. From the Western perspective, a huge majority of cultures in other parts of the world digress from the model responses when receiving praises or compliments. However, Wierzbicka (1991) further argues that this perception is rather peculiar and bias. Her argument continues,

"If a large proportion of compliment responses 'deviate from the model' of accepting compliments, then is it not perhaps the model which is inadequate? Shouldn't one rather speak of a number of different models, operating in different cultures and subcultures?"

(Wierzbicka, 1991, p.144)

Hence, the compliment response in Iban culture reflects no deviation of the model, but simply an instance of a different cultural model. Besides, it is the Iban cultural norm to response to compliments in such a way. By using NSM, we could explicate this phenomenon of compliment response as follows:

deflection of remarks on receiving a compliment:
X thinks something like this (about Y):
when I feel something
I don't want to say how I feel to Y
I will say something else to Y because of this
I will say something like this:
I don't think the same
I think that something about it (my Z) is bad
I think Y will know how I feel
X feel like this

In relation to the expression of 'thank you', *gaga* and *andal* are another two expressions of good feeling, which are used interchangeably in the Iban language; they are closely glossed as 'happy', 'glad', 'delightful' and 'gay' in bilingual dictionaries. Some examples of the expressions are provided in the following:

1. *Sida ia **gaga** amai ati meda penatai bala temuai.*
   (They are happy to see the guests coming.)
2. ***Andal** ati apai enggau indai ia laban ia udah pas ba peresa perintah.*
   (His parents are delightful because he has passed his public examination.)

The following explication illustrates the state of *gaga* or *andal* in Iban:

gaga/andal
X feels something like this:
>something good happens in me
>not because I don't want it
>because of this, I want you to know that I feel something good
>not because I say it
>if you can see me, you will know how I feel

because of this, X feels something good

The Social Expression of *Minta Ampun* or 'Sorry'

The reluctance of the Ibans to verbalize their emotional feelings can also be seen in their expression of 'guilt'. When someone has done something bad to someone else, it would be difficult for that person to express verbal utterances, such as "I'm sorry, I was wrong". Instead, the person normally resorts to a strategy, which is to be extra nice to the person. If the person has to say something, the verbal expression would be vague and there would be no direct reference to the offended person's feeling (which conforms to the restriction in the Iban culture to verbally express personal feelings). Notably, there is no exact word for 'apology' in Iban. As identified by Howell (1908, p.16), "apologies are not accepted" in the Iban ethnic, which further conforms to the non-existence of the verbal expression. The following explication is presented to illustrate this phenomenon:

X thinks something like this:
I know I did something bad to Y
>it is bad for me to do something like this
>I feel something bad towards Y because of this
>I know: Y feels something bad for me because of this
>I want Y to feel something good not because I say it
>if Y can see me, Y will know how I feel

because of this, X feels something bad

However, due to the influence of Malay and English, most Iban people nowadays tend to use *minta ampun* and 'sorry'. Nevertheless, although 'sorry' is used to denote the expression of 'guilt', it does not correspond to the English intention of displaying one's own regrets. Instead, the term 'sorry' brings out the meaning of 'to comfort' or 'to console', which is an act that will make the person feel better. Thus, the expression of 'sorry' or *minta ampun* can be further explicated as follows:

sorry/*minta ampun*
X thinks something like this:
    I know I did something bad to Y
    it is bad for me do something like this
    I feel something bad towards Y because of this
    I know: Y feels something bad towards me because of this
    I say this because I want Y to feel something good
because of this, X feels something bad

The Emotion Expression of *Tekenyit* or *Abis Ati*

The terms *tekenyit* and *abis ati* are synonyms, which are closely translated as 'shocked' or 'surprised' in English dictionaries. However, the term 'surprised' in English is normally used to describe the emotional feeling when one is granted with a pleasant experience, such as on being visited by a long lost friend or relative, being given a birthday party without one's knowledge, and so forth. On the contrary, *tekenyit* or *abis ati* in Iban is normally used to convey the feeling of unpleasantness, such as upon receiving a bad news when someone close has passed away, being betrayed by a person who one had really trusted, and the like. In other words, the expression is a spontaneous reaction to things or circumstances that occur not of one's readiness or willingness. Some examples of the expression are as follows:

1. ***Abis ati*** *apai-indai ia ninga rita ia ti udah nadai.*
    (His parents are struck by the news that he has passed away.)

2. *Kami **tekenyit** ninga rita jai nya.*
   (We are shocked to hear the bad news.)

The following explication illustrates the terms:

tekenyit/abis ati
X feels something like this:
    something bad happens in me, not because I want it
    I can say something about myself because of that
    wanting to cause someone to be able to imagine it:
        imagine that something you've wanted to be sayable
        about something is not going to be sayable about it
    because of this, I want you to know that I feel something bad
        not because I say it
    if you can see me, you will know how I feel
because of this, X feels something bad

The Social Emotion of *Buyan*

Buyan is a personal feeling that conveys a negative connotation to any Iban person. It is closely translated as 'scared', 'frightened,' or 'coward'. However, unlike the English terms 'scared' and 'frightened', *buyan* brings out negative reactions to the personal feeling, not only from the person himself, but also from others. This is due to the fact that in Iban culture, it stresses the warrior code of conduct, which means that, it is expected of any Iban (either male or female) to have the attributes of bravery and courage in him or her, especially during headhunting. Furthermore, the courage in headhunting would determine a male's manhood in Iban, as well as signify that he is not *buyan* (coward). A *buyan* person is normally seen as useless, which will result in the rejection of his being. To be marked or recognized as one will cause an extreme disgrace and humiliation to the person.

Anything can cause a person to feel *buyan*, such as darkness, a thunderstorm, loneliness, thoughts of ghosts, and so forth. Below are examples of utterances using the expression:

1. ***Buyan*** *amai anak di' nya, diasoh aku ngambik utai ke bilik enggai meh.*
    (Your child is really a coward, he refuses to fetch things from the room even though I've told him to do so.)
2. *Enggai ka dikumbai urang* ***buyan***, *ia lalu ngejang nitih ka bala ia ngayau.*
    (Scared of being called a coward, he hurriedly followed the headhunting party.)

The following explication illustrates the term *buyan:*

buyan
X feels something like this:
> something bad happens in me
>> not because I want it
>>> I can say something about myself because of that
> because of this:
>> I know this person can feel something bad about me
>> I know this person can think something bad about me
>> I know this person can say something bad about me
X feels something bad

Facial Expressions as a Means of Expressing Emotions

Izard (1979) states that non-verbal expressions communicate messages that are crucial in human social interaction. Facial expressions inform us of one's emotional state—whether he or she is happy or sad, angry or frightened, surprised or shy. Indisputably, there are cross-cultural differences in attitudes towards emotion expressions. For a culture which highly depends on non-verbal messages, the expressions of non-verbal behaviour become an important means of communicating emotional feelings.

In Iban culture which discourages the people from verbally displaying their emotions, facial expressions take the primary means of communication. Due to this restriction, it is expected of everyone to be sensitive to the facial expressions of other people. Hence, this confirms the fact that in Iban concrete or high context culture, verbal expression is a secondary means of expressing emotions. Instead, expression of emotion is conveyed through sensitivity to other people's body language and facial expressions. This circumstance can be explicated as follows:

X thinks something like this:
    when I feel something
    it is not good to say something like this to another person:
        'I feel like this'
    if the other person can see me, he/she will know how I feel

More often, when one is *pedis ati, ransi, ringat, kudi, gaga, malu* and so forth, one tends to give signals of non-verbal expressions, such as by giving a 'meaningful look'. For example, when someone has caused annoyance to a person, the strategy used is by glaring at the person in order to convey his or her irritated feeling with the person's behaviour. This is often the means used when a child misbehaves. By widening the eyes, one can also give out signals of irritation or disapproval.

With regard to the terms *sayau* and *rindu* (closely translated as 'love' in bilingual dictionaries), these emotional feelings are normally not uttered. In Iban culture, when one wishes to express one's feeling of affection or love to someone else, words of intimacy are typically not articulated. Instead, facial expressions, such as eye contact and presentation of gift(s), are used. Thus, messages of love or affection are conceived and internalized in the non-verbal behaviours. Besides, one will also resort to indirect speech acts in order to convey one's love to someone. Nevertheless, the terms *sayau* and *rindu* can be explicated in the following two ways:

(i) expression of *sayau/rindu* by means of non-verbal acts:

> X thinks something like this:
> > something good happens in me
> > > not because I don't want it
> >
> > I feel something good about myself because of that
> > I feel something good towards Y because of this
> > I want Y to know that I feel something good towards Y
> > > not because I say anything about it
> >
> > if Y can see me, I think Y will know how I feel
>
> X feels something good

(ii) expression of *sayau/rindu* by means of indirect speech acts:

> X thinks something like this (about Y):
> > something good happens in me
> > > not because I don't want it
> >
> > I feel something good towards Y because of this
> > I want Y to know that I feel something good towards Y
> > I don't want to say how I feel to Y
> > I will say something else to Y because of this
> > I think Y will know how I feel
>
> X feels like this

Similar to the expressions of *sayau* and *rindu*, the expressions of *lelengau* and *seilu-ilu* (closely translated as the 'feelings of missing someone') are also unverbalized in Iban culture. *Lelengau* and *seilu-ilu* denote the feelings of sadness upon missing the loved ones. The following explication illustrates the emotion terms:

lelengau/seilu-ilu
X thinks something like this:
    something sad happens in me
        not because I want it
    I feel something sad about myself because of that
    I feel something sad towards Y because of this
    I want Y to know that I feel something sad towards Y
        not because I say anything about it
    if Y can see me, I think Y will know how I feel
X feels something sad

The restriction of verbal expression also applies to the expression of *kasih* or *sinu* (the feeling that is connected with 'sympathy' or 'sorry'). The expression normally denotes one's personal emotion upon seeing others' misery, distress, grief or bad luck. When one feels *sinu* or *kasih* to someone else, it is unlikely for the person to express his or her emotion verbally. Again, the use of facial expression is preferred. In addition, one also tends to say something else in order to make the person feel better. The emotion expression can be explicated in the following ways:

(i) X thinks something like this (about Y):
      something sad happens in me
            not because I don't want it
        I feel something sad about myself because of that
        I feel something sad towards Y because of this
        I want Y to know that I feel something sad towards Y
            not because I say anything about it
        if Y can see me, I think Y can feel something good
      X feels this

(ii) expression of *sinu/kasih* by means of indirect speech acts:
      X thinks something like this (about Y):
        something sad happens in me
            not because I don't want it

> I feel something sad towards Y because of this
> I want Y to know that I feel something sad towards Y
> I don't want to say how I feel to Y
> I will say something else to Y because of this
> because of this, I think Y can feel something good
> X feels like this

The use of non-verbal expressions also confirms to the Ibans' strong sense of belonging in the community. This means that the people understand one another even though the messages of interaction are not uttered; they are, however, conceived in the non-verbal codes. D'Cruz and Steele point out (2000) that group members of the more concrete cultures (such as those in the Iban ethnic) share a sense of belonging, which is fundamental to human need. The researchers continue stating that, human beings comprehend speech acts without having to provide clarifications, whereby,

> "[human] gestures, words, all that enters into communications, is grasped, without mediation by members of [the] society'; and that is 'language, habits, gestures, instinctive reactions, that create unity and solidarity—distinctive outlooks, cultures, social whole'"
>
> (D'Cruz & Steele, 2000, p.93)

Often, members of closely related groups, such as the Ibans, experience this transparency—an encounter which members of the more abstract cultures or unrelated/stranger groups lack. Levi-Strauss and Eribon (1991, as cited in D'Cruz & Steele 2000, p.93) comment that,

> "[t]he mind of the more concrete person, . . . works by the opposite of the Cartesian method; it refuses to break the difficulty into parts, never accepts a partial answer, and seeks explanations that encompass the totality of phenomena".

Indirectness as a Rule of Speaking among the Ibans

According to Saville-Troike (1993, p.154),

"the rule for interaction components includes an explanation of the rules for the use of speech which are applicable to the communicative event. By 'rules' in this context, [it refers] to prescriptive statements of behaviour, of how people 'should' act, which are tied to shared values of the speech community. They may additionally be descriptive of typical behaviour, but this is not a necessary criterion for inclusion in this component. How, and the degree to which, this 'deal' is indeed 'real' is part of the information to be collected and analyzed, along with the positive and negative sanctions which are applied to their observance or violation. The rules may already be codified in the form of aphorism, proverbs, or even laws. Or they may be held unconsciously and require more indirect elicitation and identification. Rules of interaction are often discoverable in reactions to their violation by others, and feelings that contrary behaviour is 'impolite' or 'odd' in some respect."

Culture determines the rules of speaking. In turn, rules of speaking decide what and how things should be uttered. Such rules serve to control community behaviours through the establishment of appropriate responses to stimuli for a particular communication context. Rules that govern the system of expected behaviour patterns are culturally and contextually bound (Samovar & Porter, 1991).

In Iban culture, as already noted, it is the norm of the people to be indirect in their style of expressing their emotional feelings. This rule of speaking generally hinders the people from verbally or indirectly expressing their emotional thoughts. Instead, while expressing their emotional feelings, such as gratitude, love and loneliness, the Ibans tend to say something else to the other person.

The rules of speaking in Iban culture require the members to be indirect in their interaction with others. In expressing their gratitude, for example, the Ibans tend to deflect the remarks given by the other speaker whenever a compliment is received. It is the norm of the Ibans to say things like *"Udah lama utai tu'. Baru deka ngena iya sari tu'."* (This is just an old thing. It is today that I want to wear it.) when someone compliments somebody on her dress, *"Gamal nya kumbai di' manah? Pemadu jai nya."* (You think this is a pretty face? She is such an ugly girl.) when someone praises the appearance of somebody's child, and so forth. Hence, we could hardly hear the Iban people to simply utter words of 'thank you' to show their feelings. This is because, in Iban culture, it is considered *lawa* (a term which is closely glossed as 'presumptuous' or snobbish') to simply succumb to compliments. To be marked as *lawa* brings a negative reputation to an Iban individual. A person referred to as *lawa* will also become the subject of humiliation and mortification in the community. Although it is understood that the receivers are gratified with the compliments, the appropriate reaction is to deflect the remarks and show humility to the other speaker. The following explication illustrates the term *lawa*:

lawa
X thinks something like this:
> when I feel something
> it is not good to say something like this to another person:
>> 'I feel like this'
> if I say 'I feel like this' to another person:
>> I know this person can feel something bad about me
>> I know this person can think something bad about me
>> I know this person can say something bad about me
> because of this, I don't want this
X feels something like this

In addition, the avoidance of being depicted as *lawa* indicates a good breeding in an Iban individual and a display of humility. This is to ensure that the individual's action will not bring *malu* (i.e. shame) to his or her being, as well as to the family and the whole community. Thus, the rules of speaking in the Iban community require one to be humble and realize one's place in a community.

In other instances, the rules of speaking in Iban culture also require them to be indirect in their expression of personal feelings in relation to affectionate expressions, such as *sayau, lelengau, kasih* and *rindu*. It is quite unlikely to hear the Iban people expressing directly their affection by saying verbal utterances, such as *"Aku sayau ka di'."* (I love you.), or *"Aku lelengau ka di'."* (I miss you.) to another person. Instead, when one wishes to convey his or her affection to someone, one tends to be indirect in one's speech by saying something else, such as *"Kini penunga di' ngelama tu?"* (Where have you been all this time?), *"Manah amai enti aku ngempu di'."* (It will be wonderful if I could own you.), and so forth. Needless to say, to be direct in one's expression will be considered as *jelah-jelah* (closely translated as 'presumptuous', 'impertinent', and 'impudent') by the other members of the group. No sensible Iban individual will want to be marked as *jelah-jelah* due to the negative reputation that the remark brings. Therefore, to avoid the remark, one tends to stick to the indirect rule of speaking in Iban culture. The expression can be explicated as follows:

> X feels something like this:
>> I feel something good towards this person
>> I want this person to know that I feel something good
>> I don't want to say 'I feel like this' to this person
>> I will say something else to this person because of this
>> I think this person will know how I feel
> X feels like this

The rules of speaking in Iban culture determine the style of interaction in the community, which govern the personal and social behaviours of an Iban person. A violation of the rules will result in negative consequences. Hence, these rules control the interactional behaviours through appropriate establishments of response to communicative events.

Borrowing as a Means of Language Acquisition in Iban

The findings of this research showed that the members of the younger generation (aged between 20 and 40 years) resorted to borrowing the Malay and English terms, such as *terima kasih, minta ampun, benchi, pedis ati*, 'thank you' and 'sorry', when conveying their emotion expressions. This could be due to the fact that the younger generation are more in contact with multi-racial people in schools, workplaces, public locations (e.g. shopping complexes), and others, which expose them to the loanwords. Moulded by the society around them, borrowing becomes an essential tool for conveying emotional thoughts. In contrast, the older generation, whose interactional and communicative behaviours are restricted to the longhouse surroundings, tend to borrow less from other languages. They are less mobile and more confined to longhouse living, which results in less exposure of loanwords in their daily interaction. Table 11 and Table 12 display the Malay and English loanwords used by the respondents. The following are some examples of loanword expressions given by the respondents:

1. *Aku meri **terima kasih** ngagai di' laban udah nulong aku.*
   (I thank you for helping me.)
2. **Thank you** *laban pemanah ati di'.*
   (Thank you for being kind.)
3. *Aku **minta ampun** enti jako aku bisi kasar mimit.*
   (I seek your forgiveness if my words are a little harsh.)
4. **Sorry**, *laban aku laun datai.*
   (Sorry for being late.)
5. ***Pedis ati*** *aku ketegal ia.*
   (I am angry because of him.)
6. ***Benchi*** *amai aku meda orang nya.*
   (I hate to see that person.)

Due to the fact that Iban and Malay are closely related, it is no surprise that the respondents tended to borrow extensively from Malay. A majority of the respondents agreed that it is more convenient to express the emotions in Malay or English, especially when it comes to the expressions such as 'guilt' and gratitude'. This is because, verbal expressions of these emotions do not exist in the Iban language.

Although there is evidence of loanwords in Iban, this does not indicate that the language has lost its importance in the community. The tendency to borrow from other languages (e.g. Malay and English) is not an indication of language loss. Instead, all the respondents agreed that the loanwords help to enhance the Iban language by adding to its vocabulary.

Apparently, the loanwords do not follow the phonological system of the languages. Through the processes of simplification and modification, the pronunciation and spelling of the loanwords are simplified and modified in accordance with the native speakers' phonological system. The following table illustrates the pronunciation of Malay and English loanwords in Iban.

Table 11: Pronunciation of Malay loanwords in Iban

Malay	Loanwords	Malay Pronunciation	Iban Pronunciation
terima kasih	terima kasih	/tərɪmə kasɪh/	/tərimaʔ kasiᵉh/
minta ampun	minta ampun	/mɪntə ampun/	/mintaʔ ampuᵉn/
kasihan	kasih	/kasɪhan/	/kasiᵉh/
benci	benchi	/bəntʃɪ/	/bəntʃiʔ/
sayang	sayau	/sajaŋ/	/sajau/
pedih hati	pedis ati	/pədɪh hatɪ/	/pədiᵉs ati/

Table 12: Pronunciation of English loanwords in Iban

English	Loanwords	English Pronunciation	Iban Pronunciation
thank you	thank you	/θæŋkiu/	/tæŋkiu/
sorry	sorry	/sɒri/	/suri/

Trager (1972), as cited in Mohamad Subakir (1992), states that, when a language takes over the loanwords from another language, there are always some modifications of the loanwords from their original in phonology and morphology. These loanwords are taken into the recipient language in two ways: (1) they may appear into forms already acceptable to the borrowing language, or (2) they may retain some alien features and introduce new phonological patterns. Thus, the loanwords in Iban can be either fully assimilated in the language, or can maintain their alien features because these features have become familiar to the speakers of Iban. Nevertheless, the pronunciation of the loanwords is altered in order to facilitate their use by the Iban speakers.

The respondents seemingly acknowledged Malay as the dominant language because of its status as the basis for national language in Malaysia, although Iban still retains its status as an important language among the people of Sarawak. Borrowing is then perceived as an important means of language acquisition by adding to the vocabulary of Iban. The Iban language is still very much a language of great importance in the life of any Iban. It is every Iban's obligation to transfer the knowledge of the language as well as the culture to the succeeding generations in order to ensure that the language will continue to serve as the language spoken by every Iban individual. At present, the subject of Iban language is included in the school curriculum in Sarawak, offered until Form Five.

Locating the Ibans' Way of Interaction on the Cultural Continuum

Although NSM plays a very important role in explicating and describing cultural ways of communication, the weakness of the analytical tool is that, it tends to divide human interaction into separate distinctive styles—either concrete or abstract. However, to underline a point briefly referred to earlier, D'Cruz and Steele (2000: 98) mention that,

"[t]here are no societies that are purely concrete or purely abstract; the end-points of a continuum are merely conceptual terminals. The notion of the continuum helps avoid what has been a common practice of marking off culture by simplistically pitting 'group-oriented' Afro-Asian cultures against 'individualistic' Western cultures . . . . One does not dichotomise pure and simple, though one could speak of being more of one orientation or more of other orientation on a continuum."

From the findings of this study, we could locate the Ibans' interactional and relational style at the more concrete end of the cultural continuum. As already mentioned in Chapter 1, members of the concrete cultures, such as the Ibans, tend to view the world from the collective angle. They have a great tendency to gear their personal and social behaviours towards the collective values and norms of the indigenous group. They also have a strong tendency to view issues in relational terms. Every action, judgement, observation and measurement of an individual is evaluated beforehand in order to avoid violation of the group's values and norms, especially the rules of *adat*. This confirms with D'Cruz and Steele (2000) (see also Kim, Sharkey & Singelis, 1994; Triandis, 1989; Condon & Yousef, 1975), who state that members of the concrete cultures tend to relate themselves to particular others especially to members of clans, ethnic groups, and so forth. Thus, the Iban members are directed towards maintaining the group's harmony and appropriateness in their relationship with others. In exchange for their loyalty, the members are given social protection by the community living in the longhouse.

The attribute of concreteness is seen in the way the Ibans utilize non-verbal behaviours as a means of expressing emotions. Messages are instead conceived in non-verbal actions, which are later internalized by other Iban receivers. Information is not coded verbally but transmitted through a continuous and imprecise non-verbal format. They also have the expectation that other members of the group are also able to understand the non-verbal articulated communication.

The concreteness of the Ibans also denotes interdependent self-construal in the individuals. Markus and Kitayama (1991, in Kim, Sharkey & Singelis, 1994) conceptualize the notion of self-concept as the degree to which individuals see themselves as separate entities from others or as connected with others. Persons with interdependent self-construal tend to emphasize the importance of group conformity. The harmony and conformity in the Iban community are accomplished with imprecise, ambiguous verbal communicative behaviours, such as evident in their ways of expressing their emotional feelings. In addition, the value orientation of concreteness constraints the Iban people from speaking boldly through their explicit verbal communicative style.

The attribute of concreteness in Iban culture is strongly reflected in their style of communication. This is evident from their choice of conversational constraint, that is, they tend to avoid hurting other people's feelings. This choice of conversational constraint is closely related to Brown and Levinson's (1978) notion of politeness, that is the speaker's perceived obligation in keeping the hearer's desire in order to seek approval or positive self-image that the hearer claims. The concrete or collectivistic Iban person is likely to emphasize this conversational constraint and tends to focus on maintaining other people's positive face by minimizing threats to their feelings. It is the Iban culture to stress politeness which is closely linked to the concepts of *adat* and *jaga mua*. The concept of *adat* makes up a major underlying element of value in the Iban people. Great care must be taken at meetings over disagreeing or criticizing, and competitive situations should be avoided in Iban culture. Hence, in their communication, the style of Iban speech acts is directed towards maintaining face value. In fact, the concern for avoiding other people's feeling in communication is to maintain group harmony as well as an indication that the Iban ethnic is a strong concrete culture.

Other evidence which signifies that the Iban community has a strong concrete culture is also found in their tendency to avoid negative evaluation by other people. The rules of speaking in Iban restrict the people from directly expressing their personal thoughts. A violation of the rules will result in negative evaluation by others. Thus, the rules control the behaviours of the Ibans and serve as a guide to appropriate personal and social behaviours. The Ibans tend to avoid any dislike, devaluation or rejection of the others. Brown and Levinson's (1978) positive politeness notion is consistent with this conversational constraint—that is, the speaker's desire to keep or maintain his or her own positive face. The concern for avoiding negative evaluation by other people is highly valued in Iban culture. The strategy is closely related to the Iban concept of *jaga mua* or face saving. In fact, this concept makes up one of the most major ethical systems of the Ibans that reflects their characters and development and is implemented in their interaction with others, either intraculturally or interculturally.

CHAPTER V
CONCLUSION

Summary

The findings obtained from the longhouse respondents reveal that the Iban emotion concepts are unique and exhaustive. Most of the Iban emotion concepts (e.g. *malu, pedis ati, ransi, kudi, ringat, lelengau, rindu,* etc.) are conveyed through non-verbal expressions, for instance, through eye contact, exchanging of gifts (upon being given something), smiling, and so forth. These communication characteristics are indication that the Iban culture leans towards the more concrete end of the cultural continuum. The Iban emotion concepts could be translated or described by using the analytical tool developed by Wierzbicka—that is Natural Semantic Metalanguage (NSM). NSM enables us to see and understand what is truly happening in the mind of the Iban people. Through NSM, we are able to see the important core values that underlie the culture of Iban, such as the notion of *adat* and the rules of speaking in the ethnic group.

By explicating the Iban emotion concepts, we could further analyze and locate the Ibans' interactional style along the abstract-concrete cultural continuum. Moreover, the subject of 'borrowing' also reveals that the Iban language has not lost its significance or importance among the Iban people of Sarawak. In fact, borrowing has become an essential means of language acquisition, whereby it adds to the vocabulary of the Iban language.

A matter of concern is that, this study was done based on my inside knowledge of being an Iban myself. Since no studies have been carried out in relation to the Iban concepts of emotions and their way of communication, I had to rely on my self-knowledge in order to interpret the data in this research. Besides, with regard to borrowing in the Iban language, no in-depth studies on borrowing have ever been conducted by any researchers in the area. In fact, there is no clear evidence which could verify who actually borrows from whom; for example, the word *benchi* or *pedis ati* could be of Iban origin, instead of merely claiming them as Malay origins. Undeniably, the Malay language is more dominant than Iban due to the fact that it is the basis for Malaysia's national language and widely used as a lingua-franca in the Malay regions. However, this does not mean that we could underestimate the Iban language. It could be that, in some instances, Malay borrows from Iban or both languages share the linguistic items. Therefore, detailed research should be conducted in the area of borrowing in order to seek the answer to the question: *Who actually borrows from whom?* For one to do this, the etymology of the words has to be traced, and this will definitely consume a great deal of time, expense and effort.

Implications of the Study

It appears that the Iban emotion explications are unique and exhaustive; they almost resemble the Malay explications (see Hazidi, 1998). Drawing from the fact that both cultures belong to the same stock of Proto Malays (Asmah, 1983), hence this implies that the Iban and Malay languages are closely related to one another.

The Iban emotion explications also imply that the language can be systematically and precisely translated using NSM, which suggests that NSM is indeed a universal theory and a tool for cross-cultural studies. At the same time, it also enables a reduction in ethnocentric bias. Subsequently, by studying the subject of emotions in Iban culture, we can further understand the way by which emotions are expressed in the ethnic group. Besides, NSM allows us to explicate the Iban emotion concepts and learn what is happening in their minds. In addition, readers could also understand the core cultural values, such as the Iban *adat*, that underlie the personal and social communicative conducts of the people.

By explaining the emotion explications in cultural terms using the concrete/abstract cultural continuum, we are able to establish that the Ibans are more concrete in their relation with others. The use of non-verbal expressions is strong evidence of concrete attribute of the ethic group, which strongly reveals that the people tend to relate themselves with the particular others in their community. The study offers us with the insight knowledge of the Ibans' world, as to how they utilize their language code in order to interact with others. The norms of non-verbal communication and the indirect rule of speaking suggest to us that the Ibans are adept at reading non-verbal messages as well as indirect remarks. What is more interesting is that, the Ibans' way of expressing emotions closely resembles the Malay culture, indicating that the Iban and Malay cultures are indeed related to one another.

Recommendations for Further Research

Although Borneo has been the subject of many studies, the area of language and culture concerning the Iban people is rarely discussed. Specifically, in the research reading, no extensive study has been carried out in the area of language and culture pertaining to this ethnic group. For instance, the area of 'borrowing' in Iban is yet to be studied; therefore, it is rather difficult to determine the origin of Iban words. Notably, Iban has always been claimed as the language that borrows extensively from Malay, which is rather unfair to underestimate the language. Perhaps, neither Iban nor Malay borrows from one another. Both languages could have shared the linguistic items, which are proto-Austronesian in origin. Hence, a detailed study on the borrowing of words should be carried out in future in order to trace the origin of words in Iban. Unless the etymology of the words is determined, the question of *"Who actually borrows from whom?"* will not be answered.

Concluding Remarks

While Natural Semantic Metalanguage enables us to explicate and unpack the cultural meanings behind the words, it tends to divide human interaction in two distinctive and polarized categories, as either concrete or abstract. However, one's interactional style cannot be simply referred as either purely concrete or purely abstract. In fact, human interaction can be said as either more of the concrete attribution or more of the abstract attribution. Nevertheless, it cannot be denied that NSM is an essential analytical tool for reducing and avoiding ethnocentric bias. The theory of NSM is indeed universal that it can also explicate precisely and accurately the Iban emotion terminologies, hence it offers valuable insights to the Iban restricted code of expression. Furthermore, with the development of the cultural continuum, the framework helps in complementing the inadequacy or weakness of NSM, as well as assists in further describing and locating human interactional style along the concrete-abstract cultural continuum. Both elements, when combined together, provide a strong analytical tool and an interpretive framework for comparative cultural studies. The Iban emotion expressions can be more fully explicated, defined and interpreted by using NSM and the concrete/abstract cultural continuum framework.

ABOUT THE AUTHOR

The author is currently attached to Universiti Teknologi MARA (UiTM), which is based in Samarahan, Sarawak, Malaysia. Her main areas of interest include Sociolinguistics and Applied Linguistics.

REFERENCES

Abu-Lughod, L. & Lutz, C. A. (Eds.). (1990). *Language and the Politics of Emotion.* Cambridge: Cambridge University Press.

Anonymous (1904). Tugong Bula (Liar's Heap). In Borneo Literature Bureau (1963). *The Sea Dyaks and Other Races of Sarawak: Contributions to the Sarawak Gazette between 1888 and 1930* (pp. 164-165). Kuching: Borneo Literature Bureau.

Asmah, Haji Omar. (1981). *The Iban Language of Sarawak: A Grammatical Description.* Kuala Lumpur: Dewan Bahasa dan Pustaka.

Asma, Abdullah. (1996). *Going Glocal: Cultural Dimension in Malaysian Management.* Kuala Lumpur: Malaysian Institute of Management.

Condon, J. C. & Yousef, F. S. (1975). *An Introduction to Intercultural Communication.* New York: The Bobbs-Merill Company, Inc.

D'Cruz, J. V. & Tham, G. (1993). *Nursing and Nursing Education in Multicultural Australia.* Melbourne: David Lowell Publications.

D'Cruz, J. V. & Steele, W. (2000). *Australia's Ambivalence Towards Asia: Politics, Neo/Post-colonialism, and Fact/Fiction.* Bangi: Universiti Kebangsaan Malaysia Press.

Freeman, D. (1970). *Report on the Iban.* New York: Humanities Press Inc.

Fromkin, V. & Rodman, R. (1993). *An Introduction to Language.* New York: Harcourt Brace College Publishers.

Goddard, C. (1997). Cultural Values and 'Cultural Scripts' of Malay (Bahasa Melayu). *Pragmatics, 27,* 183-201.

Goddard, C. (1998). *Semantic Analysis: A Practical Introduction.* New York: Oxford University Press.

Gomez, E. H. (2004). *Seventeen Years among the Sea Dyaks of Borneo.* Kota Kinabalu: Natural History Publications (Borneo).

Hazidi, Haji Abdul Hamid. (1998). *Communicating Meaning Across Cultures.* Bangi: Universiti Kebangsaan Malaysia.

Hofstede, G. (1994). *Culture and Organization: Software of the Mind.* London: Harper Collin Business.

Howell, W. (1908). The Sea Dyaks. In Borneo Literature Bureau. (1963). *The Sea Dyaks and Other Races of Sarawak: Contributions to the Sarawak Gazette between 1888 and 1930* (pp. 13-16). Kuching: Borneo Literature Bureau.

Howell, W. (1909). The Sea Dyaks Religion. In Borneo Literature Bureau. (1963). *The Sea Dyaks and Other Races of Sarawak: Contributions to the Sarawak Gazette between 1888 and 1930* (pp. 17-23). Kuching: Borneo Literature Bureau.

Howell, W. (1910). Tugong Bula (Liar's Heap). In Borneo Literature Bureau. (1963). *The Sea Dyaks and Other Races of Sarawak: Contributions to the Sarawak Gazette between 1888 and 1930* (pp. 166). Kuching: Borneo Literature Bureau.

Izard, C. E. (1979). Facial Expression, Emotion, and Motivation. In Wolfgang, Aaron (Ed.), *Nonverbal Behaviour: Applications and Cultural Implications.* New York: Academic Press.

Jensen, E. (1974). *The Iban and Their Religion.* Oxford: Clarendon Press.

Kedit, P. M. (1980). *Modernization Among the Iban of Sarawak.* Kuala Lumpur: Dewan Bahasa dan Pustaka.

Kim, Min-Sun, Sharkey, W. F. & Singelis, T. M. (1994). The Relationship between Individuals' Self-Construals and Perceived Importance of Interactive Constraints. *International Journal of Intercultural Relations.* 18, 117-140.

Lim, P. C. (1989). *Among the Dayaks.* Singapore: Graham Brash.

Metcalf, P. (1996). Images of Headhunting. In Honskins, Janet. (Ed.), *Headhunting and the Social Imagination in Southeast Asia* (pp. 265-280). Stanford: Stanford University Press.

Mohamad Subakir, Mohamad Yasin. (1998). *Language Allegiance and Language Shift.* Bangi: Universiti Kebangsaan Malaysia.

Mohamad Subakir, Mohamad Yasin. (1992). Javanese Loanwords in Malay (Working papers in Linguistics). Manoa: University of Hawaii' at Manoa.

Porter, R. E. & Samovar, L. (1991). *Intercultural Communication.* California: Wordsworth Publishing.

Richards, A. (1981). *An Iban-English Dictionary.* Oxford: Clarendon Press.

Sandin, B. (1967). *The Sea Dayaks of Borneo: Before White Rajah Rule.* Michigan: Michigan State University Press.

Sandin, B. (1980). *Iban Adat and Augury.* Penang: Penerbit Universiti Sains Malaysia.

Sapir, E. (1961). In Blount, B. G. (1974). *Language, Culture and Society* (46-66). Cambridge, Massachusetts: Winthrop Publisher, Inc.

Saville-Troike, M. (1993). *The Ethnography of Communication: An Introduction.* Oxford & Cambridge: Blackwell Publisher.

Sutlive, V. (1994). *Handy Reference Dictionary of Iban and English.* Kuching: Tun Jugah Foundation.

Triandis, H. C. (1989). The Self and Social Behaviour in Differing Cultural Contexts. *Psychological Review,* 96 (3), 506-520.

Triandis, H. C., Brislin, Richard & Hui, C. H. (1988). Cross-Cultural Training across the Individualism-Collectivism Divide. *International Journal of Intercultural Relations,* 12, 269-289.

Wazir, J. K. (Ed.). (1990). *Emotions of Culture: A Malay Perspective.* Singapore: Oxford University Press

Wierzbicka, A. (1980). *Lingua Mentalis: The Semantics of Natural Language.* Sydney: Academy Press.

Wierzbicka, A. (1991). *Cross-Cultural Pragmatics: The Semantics of Human Interaction.* New York: Mouton de Gruyter.

Wierzbicka, A. (1992). *Semantics, Culture, and Cognition: Universal Human Concepts in Culture-Specific Configurations.* New York & Oxford: Oxford University Press.

Wilkinson, R. J. (1958). A Malay-English Dictionary (Romanised). London: Macmillan & Co. Ltd.

Winstedt, R. (1967). *A Practical Modern Malay-English Dictionary.* Fourth Edition. Kuala Lumpur-Singapore: Marican & Sons (Malaysia) Ltd.

Yule, G. (1993). *The Study of Language.* Cambridge: Cambridge University Press.

APPENDIX A

Interview Questions

1. **Anger/Shame/Surprise/Disgust**
   Situations:

   a. How would you react if someone hurts your feeling and does not bother to apologize?
   b. How do you react when you find out that someone you really trust betrays you?
   c. Someone humiliates you in front of somebody (e.g. say nasty things about you), how do you describe your feeling at that moment?

2. **Gratitude/Joy**
   Situations:

   a. How do you express your gratitude when someone has just granted you a favour?
   b. Someone has given you something (e.g. food, a souvenir, money), what is/are the word/words that you use to describe your gratitude towards her/him?
   c. You have just won a competition. How do you describe your feeling at that moment?
   d. Someone compliments your dress. What is your immediate response to the situation?

3. **Love/Affection**
   Situations:

   a. How do you express your affection to someone you love?
   b. You really fancy someone. How do you describe your feeling for her/him?
   c. How do say 'I love you' in Iban?

4. **Loneliness**
   Situation:

   a. You have not seen your loved one for a long time and you terribly miss her/him. How do you describe your feeling at that moment?

5. **Guilt**
   Situations:

   a. You realize you have hurt someone's feeling. How do you make up with her/him?
   b. How do you say 'I am sorry' in Iban?

6. **Sympathy**
   Situations:

   a. Your close friend has received a bad news. How do you feel towards her or him?
   b. You come across an old beggar with an amputated leg. How do you feel towards him?

7. **Attitude towards Loanwords**
   Situations:

   a. What is your attitude towards the Iban language borrowing from other languages (e.g. Malay and English)?

GLOSSARY OF IBAN WORDS AND PHRASES

A

abis ati—this emotion term is closely translated as 'shocked or 'surprised' in English dictionaries; it is normally used to convey feelings of unpleasantness, such as upon receiving a bad news when someone close has passed away.

adat—this term refers to the complex 'rules of logic' in Iban, which cover a wide range of various customary norms, judicial rules, and ritual injunctions that guide an Iban member's code of conduct; *adat* also comprises sanctions and forms of redress by which these norms and rules are upheld.

andal—this emotion term is closely glossed as 'happy', 'glad', 'delightful' and 'gay' in bilingual dictionaries.

antu pala—the enemies' heads taken as trophies or tokens during headhunting

B

baum—a general meeting held by the Iban community

bebulu ati—this term is an emotional expression that is closely related to the expression of 'anger' in Iban, which also denotes a strong version of anger.

beburong—an act of formal auguries in the Iban culture and traditions

bebendai—this is one of the valuable brassware in the Iban longhouse, which serves many functions, for instance, as a wedding gift in the traditional Iban culture and as a musical percussion instrument hit with a mallet during Iban festival ceremonies

bedurok—an Iban community system of labour-exchange in paddy farming that involves collaborative work groups on a labour-exchange basis

begedi—the term is an emotional expression which refers to a strong version of 'anger' in Iban

belaboh padi pun—the annual planting of the 'sacred rice'

benchi—this term is another emotional expression in Iban that denotes a mild version of 'hatred'.

bilik—an Iban family apartment unit in the longhouse

Bunsu Ribut—the god of the wind in Iban mythology

burong—this term has the primary meaning of bird; in the Iban culture and traditions, it is applied more abstractly to augural birds.

buyan—this term is closely translated as 'scared', 'frightened' or 'coward' in English.

G

gaga—this term is closely glossed as 'happy', 'glad', 'delightful' and 'gay' in bilingual dictionaries.

gawai—a festival in Iban

Gawai Antu—also known as the 'Festival of the Dead', it is an Iban feast especially attributed to the deceased that constitutes the memorialization rituals for the dead

Gawai Dayak—also called as the 'Dayak Harvest Festival', this ceremony is celebrated annually on June 1 by all the dayaks (i.e. the Iban, Bidayuh, Kayan, Kenyah, Kelabit and Murut ethnic groups) in Sarawak, as well as West Kalimantan, which marks the end of the rice harvest

Gawai Kenyalang—translated as the 'Hornbill Festival', the ritual ceremony is also associated with rice harvest celebration, which is usually held after the *Gawai Dayak* festival; in the old Iban traditions, this festival was exclusively celebrated for warriors who had killed their enemies during wars or headhunting expeditions

I

ilang—a special knife which was used as a war weapon during the headhunting days

J

jaga adat—a concept related to morality in Iban, that is to be mindful of one's manners in the public domain

jaga mua—a concept of face saving in Iban, which is compatible to the English concepts of 'dignity', 'self-respect', and 'pride'

jelah-jelah—a term which is closely translated as 'presumptuous', 'impertinent' and 'impudent' in English

K

kasih—this term is connected with the emotional feeling of 'sympathy'; it normally denotes one's personal emotion upon seeing other's misery, distress, grief or bad luck

kayau—the headhunting practice in the ancient Iban traditions

kudi—the term *kudi* indicates a strong version of anger in Iban

L

lawa—a term which is closely glossed as 'presumptuous' or 'snobbish'

lelengau—this term of emotional expression is associated with personal affection for someone; it is the feeling of missing the loved one

M

malu—this term of emotion is closely akin to the feelings of 'shame', 'modesty' and 'propriety'

minta adat—to ask for *adat*

P

pelabuh—a hut that functions as a store for keeping personal belongings

penghulu—the local district leader of the Ibans who acts as the chief of several longhouses in his region

penyalah—a term closely glossed as 'a wrongful act' in bilingual dictionaries

pedis ati—the term indicates a mild version of anger; it is an unpleasant reaction to the perception that someone has done something wrong

petara—'god' in Iban

Petara Kebong Langit—the god of the heavens in Iban mythology

Petara Puchok Kayu—the god of the trees in Iban mythology

Petara Tengah Tanah—the god of the earth in Iban mythology

pua kumbu—a traditional and special hand-woven warp or blanket, with traditional designs and motifs that depict the epitome of the Iban culture and traditions

R

ransi—the term is seemingly equivalent with 'angry' in English; it also indicates a mild version of anger in Iban

rindu—the term is also closely translated as 'love' in bilingual dictionaries

ringat—this emotion term indicates a mild version of anger in Iban

ruai—a common corridor in a longhouse that functions as a communal hall for the community formal and social gatherings

S

sampi—the word for 'prayer' in the Iban language

sayau—this term is closely translated as 'love' in bilingual dictionaries

seilu-ilu—this term is closely translated as the feeling of missing someone in Iban

Selampandai—the creator of man according to Iban mythology

Sempulang Gana—the principal god of the paddy cult in Iban mythology

Singalang Burong—depicted as the god of war in Iban mythology; he holds the utmost power among all the gods, and the Ibans believe that he possesses the prime charge over prophetic communication between the deities and mankind; it is also believed that he is responsible in releasing the omen birds to the world of humans

sinu—this emotion word is connected with the term 'sorry'; it normally denotes one's personal emotion upon seeing other's misery, distress, grief or bad luck

T

tanju—an open space or walkway on which the paddy is fanned and placed immediately under the direct sun after harvest before being stored

tawak—similar like the *bebendai*, the *tawak* is also one of the valuable items in an Iban *bilik* that functions as a wedding gift in a traditional Iban marriage custom and as a musical percussion instrument hit with a mallet during Iban festival ceremonies

tuai rumah—the headman of a longhouse who is responsible in superintending the welfare of the community under his jurisdiction; he is also the judge in matters of spiritual practice and social justice

tuak—the Iban rice wine

tugong bula—a liar's heap, which is a pile of sticks or branches that testifies a person's untruthfulness for succeeding generations to witness; it is a form of punishment for the notorious liar in memory of the person; the Iban culture considers a lie as one of the most disgraceful offences

tunggu—an Iban fine, which is a reparation payable to the injured or offended party

tusun tunggu—an Iban fine list that characterises a reparation payable to the injured or offended party

ukum—an imposed fine or a penalty

INDEX